The Rise of Benllech as a Seaside Village

Emyr Roberts

Copyright © 2020 Emyr Roberts

All rights reserved, including the right to reproduce this book, or portions thereof in any form. No part of this text may be reproduced, transmitted, downloaded, decompiled, reverse engineered, or stored, in any form or introduced into any information storage and retrieval system, in any form or by any means, whether electronic or mechanical without the express written permission of the author.

The views expressed in this work are solely those of the author and do not necessarily reflect the views of the publisher, and the publisher hereby disclaims any responsibility for them.

ISBN: 9798649424097

PublishNation
www.publishnation.co.uk

In memory of my Nain, Ellen Mary Rowlands (1887-1986), and my Aunt, Enid Huws Rowlands (1922-2003), Awelon, Ty'n-y-gongl, who looked after many visitors to the area.

Dedicated to the people of Benllech - past, present and future.

CONTENTS

Introduction

Background 1

The Nineteenth Century 5

A Rising Watering Place 33

Benllech and the First World War 61

A Well Established Seaside Resort 81

The Legacy 105

Bibliography 109

INTRODUCTION

This book traces the growth of the village of Benllech, Anglesey, from a rural and impoverished backwater during the 1800s into a popular, bustling seaside resort at the beginning of the twentieth century. This transformation took place over a number of decades, though it accelerated during the early 1900s and continued afterwards.

The Rise of Benllech as a Seaside Village largely covers the era up until the Second World War and complements my earlier book *Bro Goronwy: Hanes Plwyf Llanfairmathafarneithaf 1870-1914*. In particular, readers who are interested in the section on the nineteenth century are referred to this publication, which contains further details of the period.

As someone who was born and brought up in Benllech during the 1960s and 1970s, and whose family come from the area, I relate closely to the developments which have taken place in the village. I recently found several postcards which were posted by holidaymakers staying at the family farm, Pant y Saer, at the beginning of the 1900s. My grandmother was one of the many in the village who provided board to visitors during the summer months, and moved out of the house and into the garage to live – Nain was well into her eighties when this finally ended, and it clearly did her no harm as she lived to the grand old age of ninety-nine. My uncle established a small caravan site on the farm in the 1960s, and supplied milk and butter to Siop y Fron in the summer. And I worked at Siop Iorwerth on the square in the mid 1970s when 'flip-flops' became fashionable, and the horses from Hewitt's Riding School would trot past twice a day.

I am extremely grateful to many people who have helped to provide information, documents and photographs for this book. They include Dewi and Rhys Jones, Llio Rhydderch, Clive Hughes, Karen Jones, Nigel Pearson, Karen Bartlett, Gill Hodkinson, Jeremy Bartlett, Margaret Williams Newsome, and Alison Brigstocke. My thanks also to the staff of the Anglesey

Archives, the Bangor University Archives, the National Library of Wales, and National Museum Wales, for their help and patience with my enquiries. I am also grateful to my wife Karen for reading the draft and for her helpful suggestions. Any factual errors are mine.

I would like to thank the following for allowing me to use their photographs:

Dewi Jones – 5, 6, 12, 33, 35, 36, 37, 38, 41.

Llio Rhydderch – 4, 11, 28, 45, 46.

Anglesey Archives – 15, 20, 29, 42, 44.

National Library of Wales – 1.

National Museum Wales – 2.

Jeremy Bartlett – 3.

Cadbury Archive, Mondelēz International – 26.

Karen Bartlett – 34.

Rhys Jones – 43.

Benllech Web – 50.

All the other images belong to the author.

Although Benllech and the surrounding district has changed a great deal since the nineteenth century, in many ways it hasn't. The area around the beach and the centre of the village would still be recognisable to those living several generations ago. The beauty of the views over Traeth Coch, Mynydd Llwydiarth and the Great Orme are the same as ever. I am grateful, as I'm sure are many others, that Benllech remains a wonderful place to live and visit.

BACKGROUND

Before turning to the rise of Benllech, it may be helpful to give a brief explanation and description of the place-names and historical features of the area.

Place-names

The name *Benllech* is believed to refer to the large capstone, or *penllech* (head-stone), which is located adjacent to a farm called *Tyddyn y Benllech*, and known as *Tyddyn Iolyn* since the 1700s. There is reference to a mill at *Penclegh* in 1352, and a wool fulling-mill (*Pandû-r Benllech*) in 1718-19. The name Benllech was applied to farms in the vicinity (*Benllech Uchaf, Benllech Isaf*) until the eighteenth century, when it began to refer to the village of *(Y) Benllech*. Historically, the village of Benllech was divided between two parishes – Llanfair Mathafarn Eithaf and Llanddyfnan, the boundaries of which followed the earlier townships, with the river *Afon y Marchogion* running between them to the sea.

Tyn-y-Gongl/Ty'n-y-gongl/Ty'nygongl derives from *Tyddyn* (cottage) *y gongl* (on the corner). It was originally the name of a farm near the junction of the roads between Pentraeth – Marianglas and Rhosfawr - Benllech, and it became synonymous with the whole area during the nineteenth century when a shop and post-office were located there.

Llanfair Mathafarn Eithaf/Llanfairmathafarneithaf – *Mathafarn Eithaf* and *Mathafarn Wion* (later Llanfeistr/Llanbedrgoch) were two townships in the commote of *Dindaethwy* during the medieval period. *Mathafarn* means 'the field of the tavern', while *Eithaf* means 'furthest', probably to distinguish it from *Mathafarn Wion*. The *Llan/Llanfair* was added later to denote the church. *Gwion* or *Gwion Goch* was a local leader and the name has survived at *Groes Wion*, on the Red Wharf side, where a cross denotes the location of an important horse market in the Middle Ages.

Rhosfawr and *Brynteg* – *Rhosfawr* is literally translated as 'big moor' and referred to an area of common land nearby which was enclosed at the beginning of the nineteeth century. *Brynteg* was a house near the crossroads which became a shop and post office and gradually replaced Rhosfawr as the name of the village.

Llanbedr-goch/Llanbedrgoch is named after the 'red church of St. Peter', which was originally built in the late sixteenth century. The 'red' probably refers to the soil in the area, as in *Traeth Coch* (Red Wharf). An older name for the village is *Llanfeistr* or *Llanfaestir*.

Bro Goronwy is the name which is sometimes used for the district. There is no precise definition, but it usually refers to the old parishes of Llanfair Mathafarn Eithaf, Llanbedrgoch, and parts of Llaneugrad, Llanfihangel Tre'r Beirdd and Llanddyfnan. The term was first used in 1904 as a name for the newly-formed literary society, *Cymdeithas Lenyddol Bro Goronwy*. Goronwy Owen was one of the most important Welsh-language poets in the eighteenth century and was reputedly born at *Y Dafarn Goch* in Rhosfawr, although there is some dispute as to the precise location of his birth.

As well as the names of the villages and hamlets, there are many unusual and unique names of farms and smallholdings in the locality which reflect the rural and topographical features of the district.

Historical remains

The prehistoric era in the area is represented by the burial tomb, or cromlech, on the raised limestone plateau above the farm of Pant y Saer Uchaf. The remains of 54 people were excavated here, along with pieces of pottery, arrowheads and flint scrapers, together with a stone cist and sherds of pottery believed to be of the Beaker period. The large capstone at Tyddyn Iolyn is also possibly of a prehistoric date.

The Pant y Saer hut group, above Pant y Saer Isaf, known locally as *Cytiau'r Gwyddelod,* was excavated in 1933, and is thought to date from the early fourth century A.D.. The most important find was a fine tinned bronze brooch from the fifth to sixth century A.D., which is kept at Oriel Ynys Môn. Regrettably, the area is now overgrown and little can be seen of the hut group.

Perhaps the most exciting recent historical finds in the district relate to the fortified enclosure at Glyn, Llanbedrgoch, which developed between the seventh and tenth centuries. The site and discoveries suggest that it may have been a trading centre with Scandinavian people. In 1998-99, the skeletons of five roughly buried humans were found at the site, and it is possible that they were the victims of a Viking attack and take-over of the settlement.

1. Pant y Saer Cromlech, photograph taken in 1897

2. Artist's impression of the Pant y Saer hut group

THE NINETEENTH CENTURY

At the beginning of the nineteenth century, Llanfair Mathafarn Eithaf was a distant area in a remote part of Wales, barely accessible to the outside world apart from adventurous travellers. One such visitor in the early 1850s was George Borrow, who wanted to visit the birthplace of the poet Goronwy Owen. In a memorable section of his book, *Wild Wales*, Borrow describes his journey to the parish. Before setting off from Bangor, the local postmaster tells him:

> *"I think you will be both tired and thirsty before you get to Llanfair, supposing you go there on foot. But what may your business be at Llanfair? It is a strange place to go, unless you go to buy hogs or cattle ... why do you go to see [Goronwy Owen's] parish, it is a very poor one."*

The publican at Pentraeth then describes 'Llanfair' as a *'poor straggling village'*. Borrow continues his journey: *'All traces of the good roads of Wales had disappeared; the habitations which I saw by the way were miserable hovels into and out of which large sows were stalking, attended by their farrows ... A desolate place was Llanfair.'* His spirits are however lifted when he is invited to tea by John Jones, the Rhosfawr miller and his wife, and he comments *'My eyes filled with tears; for in the whole course of my life I had never experienced so much genuine hospitality.'*

Population

For most of the century, the district was almost totally dependent on agriculture, with some quarrying and stone masonry, while a number of men earned a living on the sea. The population grew substantially at the beginning of the 1800s and was then maintained at around 700 inhabitants until the First World War.

People lived mostly in scattered farms and *tyddynnod* (smallholdings) – there was no 'village' of any size. There were small hamlets in Rhosfawr, Ty'n-y-gongl and Benllech – of these, Ty'n-y-gongl was by far the most important, with the main shop and post office for the area; Benllech itself would not begin to grow until much later.

Despite the apparent stability, there was a regular out-migration of young people. Large numbers went to Liverpool - many of the men went into the building trade there, while most of the young women went into domestic service. Others went to the South Wales coalfields, while some of the more adventurous emigrated to the United States and other countries.

The area was overwhelmingly Welsh-speaking – in 1891, over 90% of the population of Llanfair Mathafarn Eithaf only spoke Welsh, and the remainder spoke both Welsh and English. There was not a single individual recorded in the census who only spoke English. It was also a very close-knit community, with the vast majority of the population being born within the parish or the nearby district.

In his evidence to the *Land Commission* in 1893, Hugh Williams of Pant y Saer, Ty'n-y-gongl, spoke of the conditions in the area:

> The children generally work at home, often for next to no wages. Very few of the parents of children who live on small farms are able to help their children when they leave home or marry. It would not be possible to pay the farm rents if proper wages were paid to the children for working. Not only do the children at home receive no wages, but the children who have left and gone into service, or to sea, or to work as carpenters in English cities, send money home to their parents to help with the farm rents and rates. Many farmers and smallholders in Anglesey would not survive if it were not for this. [Translated]

He also described the daily sustenance of people:

Bread and milk for breakfast; potatoes and milk, potatoes and butter, and some salted meat, for dinner; tea and buttered bread for tea; and porridge and milk for supper. Many farmers do not eat fresh meat from one year to the next. [Translated]

Land Ownership

The land in the district was mainly owned by the major landowners of Anglesey and North Wales, several of whom had inherited and acquired huge estates. In the 1840s, over three-quarters of the land in Llanfair Mathafarn Eithaf belonged to eleven of the biggest landowners, including the Bulkeley family of Baron Hill, Beaumaris, and the Meyrick family of Bodorgan. There was, however, no dominant landowner in the area, and no grand house to compare with Plas Gwyn in Pentraeth, or Parciau in Llaneugrad.

The tenant famers were of two main types – full-time farmers who used family labour and often employed a servant, and smallholders or *tyddynwyr* who lived in cottages with a small field or two and usually had another occupation. The farms in the district included:

Fferam: Fferam was one of the largest farms in the area, covering some 90 acres, and was part of the Baron Hill estate. The Fferam land was later divided up and the Fferam, Rhianfa, Garreglwyd, Bay View, and Breeze Hill housing estates were built upon it.

Tyddyn Iolyn: 22 acres, again owned by the Baron Hill estate. The Tyddyn Iolyn land became the core of the expansion of the village of Benllech.

Maes Llydan: 10 acres and owned by Lord Boston. It was farmed by William Rowlands, who was a carpenter and also a bone setter.

Pen llech or Benllech: some 21 acres, alongside the road down to the beach. Most of this area later became the location of Hewitt's caravan site.

Mynachlog: Mynachlog was a large farm of some 62 acres which was later subdivided and the Craig y Don and Refail Newydd estates were built upon it.

From the 1880s onwards, the large landowners began to auction their holdings in the area; many farms were also sold privately, often to the sitting tenants. Perhaps the most important sale of this period was in September 1886, when Tyddyn Iolyn and parts of Ben llech and Fferam were sold in lots. In many ways, this sale led to the future shape of Benllech as a village. The potential of the area as a seaside resort was highlighted in the sale catalogue:

> 'Parts of Ben llech and Fferam: Two Cottages, Warehouse, Yards, Crofts &c – This Lot is situated in a beautiful spot, and runs down to a fine sandy beach. There is very good sea fishing to be had here, and the bathing is superb'. The 'crofts' were a group of small cottages at the bottom of the road which were demolished in the 1890s. The 'warehouse and yards' were occupied by John Prydderch Williams of Siop Ty'n-y-gongl and used to store coal and goods.

> 'Parts of Tyddyn Iolyn: 8 Building Sites fronting the road' – including 'a charming Building Site which runs down to the sea shore ... grand views'.

> 'Parts of Fferam and Ben llech: The farm comprises land of excellent quality, and portions of it would make splendid sites for the erection of villa and other residences'.

The Tyddyn Iolyn building plots were alongside the main street of Benllech and became the sites for the new houses, apartments and shops for the emerging seaside resort. The corner site was bought by the schoolmaster John Williams, and he commissioned the Bangor architect Richard Davies to build Gwynfryn, which later became the Gwynfryn Hotel and is now The Benllech.

Parts of Fferam were also sold off for houses in the late 1800s; two of the most imposing were Breeze Hill, which was built for the sea captain Louis Roberts, and Garreglwyd which was built for draper Richard Edward Williams of 'Devon House', Bangor. Both later became private boarding houses and subsequently hotels.

Farming

The land in the area was generally of poor quality and the farms were small, even by Anglesey standards. It was common practice to spread seaweed and sand from the local beaches on to the land to improve its fertility. The district was largely self-sufficient and self-contained, with most agricultural products being traded at local markets and fairs, of which Llanerchymedd and Llangefni were the largest.

Farmers and smallholders would work together during the busy times of the year, especially when harvesting hay and threshing. The women and servants produced butter and collected eggs for sale. Pigs were sent to the slaughterhouse at Pentraeth, and there was another abattoir and woollen mill at Moelfre. A horse fair was held at Rhosfawr, while ploughing competitions were very popular in the area.

Agricultural labourers were employed for six or twelve months at 'hiring fairs' in Llangefni – the workers were required to line up below the town clock to be 'inspected' by prospective employers. A deal was struck on the spot, and usually a small payment (*ernes*) was made by the farmer to the worker to bind the arrangement. In the early 1900s, workers were paid £13 for six months.

In reality, there was little difference between the standard of living of the farm labourers and the small tenant famers, and distinctions of 'social class' appeared to be much less acute than in other areas.

Crafts and other industries

The agricultural community was supported by a large number of craftsmen and women – in 1841 there were 6 millers, 6 carpenter/joiners, 5 shoe/clog makers, 4 weavers, 4 blacksmiths, 2 wheelwrights, and 1 carter in Llanfair Mathafarn Eithaf. There were several windmills in the district, of which only the remains of the Rhosfawr mill can be seen today.

One family was particularly well-known as tailors and served the whole of the island. Edward Parry and his son John Charles (J.C.) Parry, Siop Tabernacl, had a thriving business serving many of Anglesey's farmers. They also dressed the gentry, including the men of the 'Anglesey Hunt', as well as the thirty or so gamekeepers who worked on the estates on the island. It took some four days to make each gamekeepers' suit, with the tailors working on each segment individually.

One of the clog makers was the Rev. Hugh Roberts, Tyddyn Tlodion, who also served as a Baptist Minister. Another of the shoemakers would take his shoes to the slate-producing town of Bethesda in Caernarfonshire on a Saturday when the wages were paid (*Dydd Sadwrn Setlo*). There were several blacksmiths in the parish who, as well as shoeing horses, would make ploughs and gates for farmers. The carpenters were also multi-skilled and could make carts, wheelbarrows and windows.

Most women worked at home in support of their families, while the younger ones were employed as servants on farms and smallholdings, often engaged in dairy work. Some also worked as dressmakers or *mantua-makers*, especially at the turn of the century when the prosperity of the area began to rise.

The area around Benllech, and especially Red Wharf, was well-known from at least the Middle Ages for producing high-quality limestone building stones and millstones. This industry continued into the nineteenth century when some 200 men worked in the quarries in the area. Several of the quarries were located along the coast, and boats would come into the bays at Benllech and Red Wharf at high tide, be loaded with the stones, and sail away at the next high tide. The remains of these quarries are visible today, especially around the 'second bay' at Benllech. Stones from the Benllech quarries were used in the construction of the Holyhead breakwater, several town halls in England and, reputedly, the lions on the entrance to the Britannia tubular bridge across the Menai Straits.

Further inland, millstones from the Bwlchgwyn quarry would be dragged by horses and mules along *y lôn dywod* (the sand road), alongside Afon y Marchogion, to the coast where they would be loaded on to boats.

Another use of the limestone was as an agricultural fertiliser. The rock would be crushed and burnt in a kiln to make quicklime. There were many lime kilns in the area, and perhaps the most well-known is the one located on the corner of the road to Red Wharf, which was later converted into a house. Apparently the kiln cracked on its first firing.

Maritime

The eastern seaboard of Anglesey has a long and illustrious maritime history and, while not as famous as the neighbouring villages of Moelfre and Traeth Coch, the area around Benllech has always had a close connection with seafaring. Almost every family had a father or son on the sea at some time, and many became master mariners on the large trading vessels. At the beginning of the twentieth century, there were at least 36 sea-captains living in the district, and many made a substantial contribution to the development of the village.

During the nineteenth century most of the basic commodities such as coal, wood, and building materials, would be brought into the area by sea, and boats would unload their freight on the open beach at Benllech where they would be collected by horse and cart.

There was also an important fishing industry in the area, particularly for herring. 'Moelfre herrings' were well-known throughout the country, and a small herring fleet operated from Benllech. The season lasted from October until February, and many sailors from the area would return home to help with the catch and supplement their incomes. Local people would travel around the island and sell the herrings off the back of a cart and horse, while others would carry them on baskets on their backs. After the railway station opened in 1909, most of the herrings were transported by horse and cart, and later lorry, to the railhead and transported to markets in Liverpool.

Some of the herring were also smoked locally and it was said that the smell of herrings being fried in Benllech and Moelfre travelled as far as the Orme's Head in Llandudno. The size of the herring catch fluctuated considerably between each season; when the large shoals were absent, blame was attributed to quarrying near the shore, or because fishing had taken place on Sundays, or that the visitors had scared them away. The herring industry in the area did not survive beyond the outbreak of the Second World War.

Housing

As the district was very poor, the standard of housing often fell well below acceptable standards. In particular, the condition of the houses of agricultural workers gave concern to the medical authorities. There were many over-crowded two-roomed cottages, with soil floors and straw roofs, as the following records from 1910 illustrate:

Pant y Sglater (1 acre) – 'Cottage having two rooms on ground floor only. Poor and insanitary condition. Pigsty. Quillet of land in front'. In 1911, John Roberts, aged 33, a 'horse servant' lived at Pant y Sglater with his wife and four children under 10 years old.

Crimach (4 acres) – 'House 25'x18' containing 2 rooms on ground floor only. Small kitchen at rear 15'x12'. Insanitary - poor floor and roof. No through ventilation. Cowhouse and barn at gable 20'x18'. Lean-to shed at rear. Pigsty in front'. Ann Jones, a widow and 'butter and eggs merchant', lived at Crimach with her daughter, son-in-law, two grandchildren and a boarder.

It was common to collect sand once a year from the beaches and to pack it onto the soil floors, so that over time the ground became rock hard. Many cottages were abandoned at the end of the century, and visitors regularly commented at the number of ruins in the locality.

Partly as a result of inadequate housing and over-crowding, contagious diseases would frequently sweep through the district – there are records of measles, whooping cough, scarlet fever, diptheria, chicken pox and especially tuberculosis affecting large numbers of the population. The epidemics were particularly harmful to children, and several deaths are recorded in the school logbooks.

Medical assistance would largely fall to local midwives who would not only help with the births, but would stay with the family for days afterwards to wash, cook and clean. They also attended the sick, and laid out the dead. If further assistance was required, a message would be carried to the doctors at Llangefni or Llanerchymedd, who would travel to attend on horseback.

There was, however, a plentiful supply of clean water from the many springs and wells in the district. It was often the job of the women and children to draw the water from the wells and to carry it home.

Roads and transport

One of the main reasons why the district was regarded as being so remote was the lack of roads into the area, and their appalling condition. The main thoroughfare across Anglesey served the port of Holyhead, and this was consolidated when Thomas Telford built the Menai Suspension Bridge in 1826. The only route of any significance to touch the district was the road from Beaumaris to Llanerchymedd, which went through Pentraeth, Llanbedrgoch and Rhosfawr – the roads into Benllech itself were no more than narrow tracks.

The lanes and paths would have been used primarily by local people to carry out their daily business, and to take animals to markets and fairs. Donkeys and mules were used to pull agricultural carts. Most people walked everywhere, while the better off would travel by pony and trap. Horse-drawn carriages or 'cars' became popular from the middle of the century for longer distances - one horse would pull a car with up to twenty-five passengers, although everyone would have to get out and walk up and down every hill. It took three hours to go to Bangor by horse-drawn car, and goods would also be carried on them to shops and workshops.

The parishes were responsible for maintaining and repairing local roads, but they were often neglected and it was not until the formation of the Anglesey County Council at the end of the century that the condition of roads in the area improved. The Council supported the building of a 'Coastal Main Road' from Menai Bridge to Amlwch to Valley. The completion of this road in 1913 would be a major turning-point in the development of Benllech.

Shops

Alongside the places of worship and the school, the local shops were the main social meeting-places for the area. Two families of shopkeepers, in particular, played key roles in the development of the village.

By far the most important shop, and the longest established, was **Siop Ty'n-y-gongl** on the crossroads between the road from Benllech to Rhosfawr and Traeth Coch to Marian-glas. The business was formed by David Williams in 1838 and he built the shop on a piece of land at Minffordd farm. When he died a few years later the shop was passed on to his nephew John Prydderch Williams and it became a Post Office in 1855. It was subsequently run by his son William Daniel (W. D.) Williams, who sub-let it to R. J. Lewis in 1911, though he retained the Post Office next door.

The shop was advertised as 'a general draper and outfitter, with dressmaking and millinery departments, grocer and provision dealer, seedsman and ironmonger, brick and tile merchant and house agent'. It was lit by oil lamps and was open from eight in the morning until eight at night, except Sundays. It sold everything from basic slag to bicarbonate of soda, including all kinds of foodstuffs, decorating materials and spades. Local women would bring baskets of eggs and butter for sale. One counter sold clothing materials and shoes, and the latest fashions would made by the dressmakers upstairs with the styles chosen from catalogues. At least seven assistants were employed there at one stage, and it provided a vigorous centre to the community. There were a number of buildings at the back, including a warehouse, coach house, stable, and a chaff room; pigs would be killed on the premises.

The Post Office moved into an extension next to the shop in 1904. The post would be delivered by eight o'clock every morning by a horse-drawn car from Menai Bridge, via Pentraeth; it would then continue to Marian-glas and Moelfre, where the carrier would have his lunch and the horse its feed, before returning to Ty'n-y-gongl by five o'clock and onwards to Menai Bridge, often carrying shoppers on the way. One of the postmen would deliver to the Rhosfawr area, while there would three others delivering to Ty'n-y-gongl and Benllech. Those working in the Post Office would often write letters on behalf of local people to be sent to relations across the world.

John Prydderch Williams and his son W. D. Williams were both extremely active on behalf of the community and very generous benefactors. The father donated the land for the Ty'n-y-gongl school and supported a host of other activities and causes. W. D. Williams was equally generous and served as County Councillor, and later Alderman, for the district for some 50 years.

The other main shop was **Y Fron** on the square at Benllech. Lewis Roberts was a master tailor and in the 1850s he moved from Ty'nygongl Bach to Y Fron. At the time, Y Fron and Pengroeslon were the only houses on the 'square'. Over time, Lewis and his wife Tryphena developed the shop from being a drapery to a grocery as well. Although Lewis Roberts died in 1890, the name continued over the shop for over a century, and was subsequently run by his wife and their daughter. Grace Roberts married Griffith Pritchard, originally a carpenter, who trained as a baker and Y Fron also became a bakery. Meetings and debates were held in the loft above the shop and it was known as the 'parliament' of the area. Siop y Fron continued largely unchanged until the late 1960s.

Lewis and Tryphena Roberts' other two daughters were also very influential in the village. Jane married Hugh William Richards, son of Michael Richards who built the Glanrafon Hotel; one of their daughters married Richard Edward Williams of Garreglwyd, who owned the Môr Annedd shop and boarding house. The other daughter Tryphena married John Williams, the Ty'n-y-gongl schoolmaster and, following his death, William Jones, the local doctor. Between them the family built and owned most of the property in the area of the square, including the Frondeg houses, Fron Uchaf and Glan Aber.

By the end of the century, other shops had also opened in the village, including Glan Dŵr. There were several small grocers in the vicinity, including Bryn Neuadd near the school in Ty'n-y-gongl.

Milk was delivered to the village and outlying areas twice a day by a milk cart; it was sold for 4d a quart and the women would come out of their houses with jugs to collect the milk. Other merchants served the area, often selling their wares from the back of a horse and cart. A butcher called from house to house each week with fresh meat and local women sold small cakes for special occasions.

During the early part of the century there were several inns and taverns in the area, including the Bignall Inn (later Tŷ Newydd, opposite Siop Ty'n-y-gongl), and Benllech Isaf. However, the strong temperance movement in the district closed many of these down and by the end of the century there was only one public house in the village - the **Glanrafon Arms**, which was established in 1865 by Michael Richards, a gamekeeper from Llaneugrad. It was rebuilt as the **Glanrafon Hotel** around 1890.

There was no electricity or phone system in the district during the nineteenth century, and it was only in 1887 that the telegraphic wires were extended from Pentraeth to Ty'n-y-gongl.

Education

The first daily schools to educate the poor of Wales in their own language were the Circulating Schools in the mid eighteenth century, and the Llanfair Mathafarn Eithaf school, normally held in the Church room, was one of the earliest to be established. However, when the Circulating Schools ended in 1779, very little was done regarding elementary education in the area apart from the work of the Sunday Schools.

A National (Church) School was established in Llanbedrgoch in 1818, a British School (Non-denominational) was built in Marianglas in 1845, and a National School was opened in Llaneugrad the following year. Attempts were made to build a British School in Llanfair Mathafarn Eithaf, but nothing came of these. Local children therefore had to trudge several miles each day along muddy footpaths and fields in order to attend the nearest daily school.

The Education Act 1870 created an opportunity for every child between 5 and 13 years old to receive an elementary education. The Ty'n-y-gongl Board School was opened on 28 January 1878 with places for up to 140 children. The building of the school was greatly helped by the donation of a piece of land on the outskirts of the village by John Prydderch Williams. The School Board took out a loan of £580 from the Public Works Board, and the school was funded through a local rate precept of £17, school fees of £18 (1d a week for each child), and a government grant of £40. The Schoolmaster was paid £75 a year, and a School House was built next door in 1885.

The school was fortunate in having two inspiring headteachers who between them led the education of the children successfully for half a century. John Williams from Holyhead was appointed in 1882 – at the beginning of his tenure he travelled at the start of each week from Holyhead to Ty'n-y-gongl on a *penny-farthing* bicycle, and back on a Friday evening. Over the next twenty years, and supported by very able assistant teachers, he raised the standard of the school so that it attracted pupils from beyond the parish. John Williams' health was fragile and he was forced to stand down in 1901; he died at his home, Gwynfryn, two years later. He was succeeded by Roland Lloyd from Beaumaris, who had previously taught at Llangefni, and who led the school with distinction for the next thirty years.

Teaching was organised into an infants class and seven *Standard* classes; there were three rooms in the school – one for the infants, one for the young children and a large room where most of the children were taught. The teaching was shared between the headmaster and two assistant teachers, and the large size of the classes and the wide range of abilities among the pupils was a constant challenge.

The children were taught through English and the curriculum was narrowly based on the three 'Rs' – reading, writing and arithmetic – although it was extended over the years. There is no evidence that the 'Welsh Not' was ever used in the school – indeed the

Schoolmasters and teachers were praised for their support of the Welsh language.

As with other elementary schools of the period, especially in rural areas, it was difficult for the authorities to ensure the regular attendance of some pupils. Children were often sent home because of the rain and poor standard of clothing and shoes, as this entry in the school log-book illustrates:

> The wet weather during the last three days has greatly affected the attendance. The fields in many places are completely flooded and the paths and lanes are submerged making it impossible for the little children to come to school. Robert Hughes and Owen Elias Hughes Tyddyn Rhedyn, William Williams Pen Y Bonc, John Thos Owen and David Owen Cytir, were so wet yesterday that they had to take off their boots to wring and dry their stockings. Several children are also laid up having contracted colds by remaining in their wet clothes.

The children regularly suffered from contagious diseases such as measles, mumps and whooping cough, and the school was frequently closed for weeks on end.

Attendance was often poor because older boys in particular were expected to work at home during the planting and harvesting seasons, or to work on neighbouring farms to supplement the household income. There were also other rural interests, such as agricultural shows, ploughing matches, otter hunts, horse races, and fairs which forced the school to close.

A school attendance officer was employed to tackle the most frequent truants and it is clear that some children received very little education:

> Ellen Owen 10 yrs of age and Mary Owen 9 were admitted this morning and although they are so old they do not know their letters properly and no arithmetic, consequently they have been put in the infant class to begin.

During the period, further education at a 'Middle School' had to be paid for, and it was therefore essential that children received a scholarship or bursary to help pay their costs. The Ty'n-y-gongl school was succesful over the years and several went on to study at the secondary schools at Beaumaris and Llangefni.

The school closed in 1969, when Ysgol Goronwy Owen opened in Benllech.

Religion

There is a long history of religious worship in the area, which was particularly strong during the nineteenth century.

St Mary's Church, Llanfair Mathafarn Eithaf dates from the medieval period, and the nave and chancel of the existing building are from that time. During the nineteenth century, the church was combined with the benefice of Llanddyfnan. In the early 1900s, the Church authorities discussed the rather remote location of the church and the desire to establish a place of worship in Benllech – it took another 50 years for this aspiration to be achieved.

It was the expansion of the Nonconformist denominations from the middle of the eighteenth century onwards which drove the religious fervour in the district. The area was one of the strongholds of Methodism in particular, and the establishment of places of worship at Waun-eura and Glasinfryn in Llanbedrgoch was the stimulus for further expansion in the locality.

Y Tabernacl (Calvinistic Methodist) was built in 1834. It was by far the largest place of worship in the vicinity, with seating for 444 people and more space to stand.

Soar, Rhosfawr (Independent) was built in 1816 and rebuilt in 1875, with seating for 150 worshippers.

Seion (Baptist) was built in 1813 and extended in 1853. It was the practice of the Ministers to baptise worshippers in the sea at

Benllech or Red Wharf and this drew large crowds, including curious visitors who had never previously witnessed such an occasion.

At the turn of the century almost every family were members of a chapel or church. Sunday Schools, which were for adults as well as children, were also very well-attended. The places of worship were a hive of activity, with 35 religious services a week held within the Nonconformist chapels alone. There were also temperance meetings, 'Band of Hope', singing festivals, Sunday School competitions, and a host of other events.

Several religious revivals occured in the area. As part of his mission to Anglesey in 1905, the evangelist Evan Roberts preached at two large-scale services at Y Tabernacl. The morning service was held indoors when some 700 attended, while the second was outdoors on the land in front of the chapel, with a congregation of between 3,000 and 3,500 people. The Ty'n-y-gongl services were celebrated as being among the most successful of the mission.

The Community

This was a very close-knit rural community, underpinned by long-established family connections, a common set of values and behaviours, and a shared need to co-operate with each other in order to survive.

The poorest members received some support from the parish in the form of 'outdoor relief' of up to 2s 6d a week. Unlike other areas, where there were several charities operating, the only beneficial cause for the poor in the district was the John Williams Charity, which exists to this day.

As nonconformism and the temperance movement were so strong in the area, it would be reasonable to assume that life was very peaceful and that people complied with the law. However, the number of court convictions (excluding drunkeness) in 1883 put the parish of Llanfair Mathafarn Eithaf as the fifth highest in the county (Llanbedrgoch was third). Most of the offences were typical of rural areas for the period and would today be regarded as minor infringements. People were convicted for trespassing in search of game, poaching, keeping a dog without a licence, allowing animals to stray on to the highway, 'driving a car furiously', and being 'drunk in charge of a horse and car'. They were mainly dealt with through a small fine.

Convictions for theft of minor items were dealt with harshly:

> John Griffith, Rhosfawr, labourer, imprisoned at Beaumaris gaol for 7 days for stealing 'certain cultivated roots, to wit 6 turnips used for the food of beasts' from William Williams, the owner of the Parciau Estate. The same landowner also prosecuted Hugh Jones, labourer, Tŷ Mawr, for taking 11 rabbits from his estate, resulting in a fine of £1 and 13s 4d costs.

> Mary Jones, servant, sentenced to one month hard labour for stealing 'one pair of stockings, one piece of curtain, one towel, one flannel petticoat, one pair of small shoes, one blanket and certain baby clothes' from Ellen Williams, Tŷ Mawr.

The community was rich in Welsh-language culture and heritage. Several *beirdd gwlad* (country poets) lived in the area, while singing, choirs and drama productions flourished. One of the most important groups was *Cymdeithas Lenyddol Bro Goronwy* (the Bro Goronwy Literary Society). The Society met every Friday evening at the Tabernacl Chapel and the events included debates, 'proxy elections', talks and concerts. The topics for debate varied from the serious political issues of the day to light-hearted topics, such as:

> - Can the present war [the Boer War] be justified?

> - Does a woman from the town or from the country make the best wife?

- Would a railway to Benllech be an advantage or a disadvantage?

- Should the Parliamentary franchise be extended to women?

Other entertainments in the district included 'magic lanterns' and later the 'cinematograph' or 'moving pictures'. Important national occasions were also celebrated:

> Queen's Diamond Jubilee – Soon after noon the children were to be seen wending their way to their respective schools. At the Board School a hearty welcome was extended to all comers, and tea and cakes were liberally dispensed ... The children, who had previously been presented with Jubilee Medals by Mr Williams Headmaster were first regaled and then marched down to the sands for games, etc. Flags were displayed everywhere and ropes of flags were stretched across the streets from the Post Office, from Gwynfryn to Mrs Roberts', and from Tynygongl farm ... All the afternoon the shore presented a most animating scene. Under the direction of Mr Williams of Gwynfryn the children sang the National Anthem and other patriotic and national songs. Donkey races and old English sports were indulged in, and the day finished by an exhibition of fireworks.

Despite the poverty and hardship, the district was a socially and culturally vibrant Welsh-speaking community during the nineteenth century. The places of religious worship, and the chapels in particular, provided a stable bedrock to the population, and the local community leaders were very active in promoting the interests of the area and its inhabitants. The opening of the first elementary school provided a massive boost to the education and prospects of children in the area. Ty'n-y-gongl was the main centre in the district, with the largest shop and post office. But towards the end of the century, the natural attractions of the area began to be recognised further afield and Benllech began to be developed for seaside holidays.

*3. Elizabeth Thomas (1811-1865), Pant y Bugail, Ty'n-y-gongl,
wearing a traditional Welsh hat and bonnet*

4. Nan Rowlands at her cottage, Marian Mawr, Marian-glas

5. Tailors from the area, with J. C. Parry on the left

6. The millstone quarry at Traeth Bychan

7. Herring boats at Y Wig

8. *Y Tabernacl, Ty'n-y-gongl, the largest chapel in the district*

9. *St. Mary's Church, Llanfair Mathafarn Eithaf*

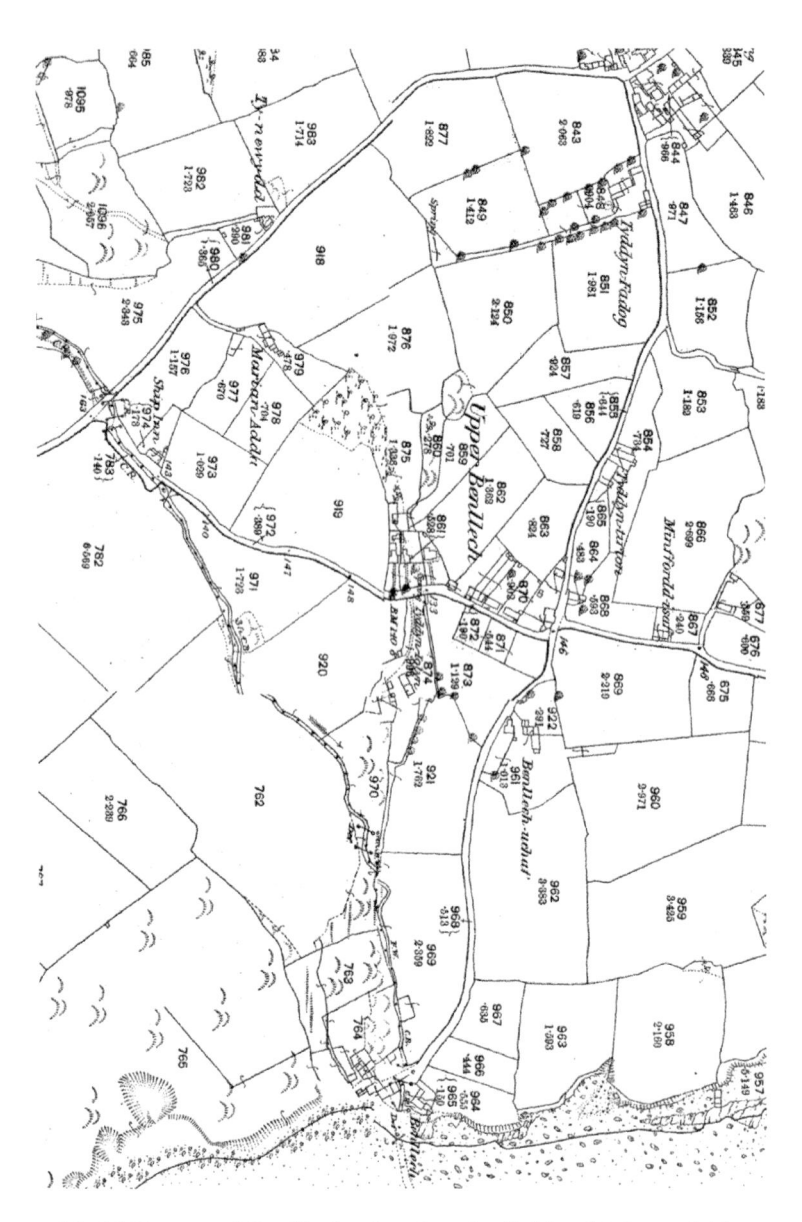

10. *1888 map of Benllech, showing the fields which would be developed later and the single track to the beach*

11. Siop Ty'n-y-gongl, early 1900s, before the Post Office was built

12. Benllech village, early 1900s

13. Benllech square, with Siop y Fron on the right

14. Milk cart coming up to Breeze Hill, with the Glanrafon Hotel on the right

15. Ty'n-y-gongl school with headmaster Roland Lloyd standing outside

16. Ty'n-y-gongl school class with John Williams, 1900

A RISING WATERING PLACE

For most of the nineteenth century, Ty'n-y-gongl was the most important 'centre' for the district with the main shop, post office, school, and the largest chapel. Brynteg also established itself as a local centre with the establishment of a general shop, post office and bakery. Benllech was a small, insignificant hamlet with a few houses along the road, half-a-dozen old cottages by the beach, and scattered houses, farms and smallholdings. However, the situation began to change at the end of the century when new houses and shops were built, and Benllech expanded. This was driven by the rising popularity of the beach and village as a seaside resort.

Early days

Visits to the British seaside became massively popular during the Victorian period as 'sea bathing' was seen as a fashionable and healthy leisure activity. This was enabled by the expansion of the railway network that opened up areas which had previously been largely inaccessible to the general public. Parts of the North Wales coast were developed, especially Llandudno which was transformed when the railway arrived in 1858 and promoted itself as 'The Queen of Welsh Resorts'. But the eastern side of Anglesey remained largely untouched, apart from Beaumaris which became well-known when the pleasure steamers called there on their day-trips from Liverpool.

There was virtually no mention of Benllech before 1890 – indeed postcards continued to call the village and beach 'Ty'n-y-gongl' for many years afterwards. Red Wharf was better-known as it had previously been a small port, and Moelfre because of the Royal Charter disaster in 1859. Even by the end the century, the publication *Seaside Watering Places* only listed Beaumaris, Holyhead, Bull Bay and Cemaes as seaside resorts on Anglesey.

However, there was an increasing awareness of the potential of the area for leisure from the early 1880s onwards. This is the advert for the sale of the Min-y-Don hotel at Red Wharf:

> It is situate within seven miles from Menai Bridge, where there is daily communication by steamer with Liverpool, and first-class railway station on the London and North Western Railway System. There is also daily communication with Bangor by cars. It is surrounded by a large and well populated agricultural district, affording abundant supply, at reasonable cost, of vegetables, milk, butter, and other necessary commodities requisite for the comfort of visitors.

Some local residents and organisations were also aware of the possibilities, and risks, of developing the area as a place to holiday. The subject of an essay competition of the district Sunday Schools was 'Benllech as a bathing-place; its advantages and disadvantages, together with the prospects for the community as a visitor destination'. Others had even higher aspirations - a public meeting held in Benllech in 1899 passed a resolution 'to establish a line of steamers to run from Liverpool to Benllech and other ports'.

The main reasons that Benllech did not attract attention during the first phase of British seaside holidays were its remoteness, the poor condition of the roads, and the lack of accommodation and infrastructure in the area. The roads remained in a shocking condition until the end of the century, and the journey by horse-drawn car from the nearest railway station at Bangor or Menai Bridge would take several hours. Few of the local houses and farms were set up to accommodate visitors. The single path to the beach from the square was steep and uneven, while there were no facilities by the beach itself.

Nevertheless, some hardy visitors did discover the area, as the following article from the *Liverpool Mercury* in 1890 illustrates:

A Welsh Summer Resort. Tyn-y-Gongl – Bathing machines are absent, but one or two umbrella tents afford shelter to their owners while dressing, and some natural clefts in the overhanging cliffs make excellent substitutes on occasion. It may be remarked, perhaps, that the sensation of performing one's toilet in the open air, with bright sunshine all around and warm winds breathing balmily over one's limbs, raises a strong suspicion in the breast that savage life is not without its attractions.

The early visitors saw themselves as adventurers, enjoying the challenge of going to remote and untouched places. It is also clear from the early reports that they were generally well-to-do and had the financial means to travel to more distant destinations. Gradually, adverts started to appear for accommodation in the area, especially in Liverpool and Manchester newspapers. Houses would be let out for the summer:

Bryn Mathafarn, Benllech Bay, Anglesey - Detached House in our Grounds, containing Spacious Hall, Sitting and Dining and Cloakrooms, Kitchen, Pantry and Scullery, Cellar, Four Spacious Bedrooms, and Two Dressing-rooms and Attic, Stable, Coach-house, and Outside Kitchen and Wash-house.

'Lodging houses' opened in the village, including Bryn Adda, Isca, Bay View, and Môr Annedd – 'the well-known Temperance Hotel and Boarding establishment'. Camping was also popular, especially in the sandhills behind the beach, St David's Bay, and above *Y Wig* (the creek).

The area around the beach was altered. Several cottages at the foot of Beach Road were demolished in the 1880s, of which only Benllech Isaf survived. Harry Walter Pritt, an iron and template merchant from Billericay, Essex (originally from Preston in Lancashire) built three imposing houses on the seafront - Glan-y-Môr, Glan-y-Don, and Brig-y-Don – which he used for his family and let out to visitors. The Ty'n-y-gongl shopkeeper, John Prydderch Williams, opened a small cabin opposite his warehouse, from which drinks and ices were sold. Boats were available to hire from Benllech Isaf and *Y Wig,* and fishing was popular.

The 'Promenade' and sea-wall were built using local stones hauled by horse-and-cart, but only reached half the distance towards the sands at the far end, with the remainder being marked by a fence. Temporary huts and tents were placed on the beach during summer to enable visitors to change into bathing clothes. A local woman remembered the scene:

> The tent was set up for a month at the beginning of the annual holiday, and within it there was a plentiful supply of buckets, spades, deck-chairs, all kinds of clothing, and cooking equipment. Large meals were produced every day and, according to my mother, nothing ever went missing during that month. [Translated]

Undoubtedly, the most luxurious place to stay in the vicinity was the Glanrafon Hotel, which was built by Michael Richards around 1890. It had all the modern conveniences and was lit by acetylene gas lamps; it boasted 'a tennis lawn, a billiard room, hot and cold baths, a special sanitary certificate and the latest interior design'. At the beginning of the century 'full board' cost 10s 6d a night or £3 13s 6d a week. During the summer months around 80 people would be staying there at any one time. John Owen, Pengroeslon, remembered working there when he was a young boy:

> The land where all the houses at Breeze Hill are now used to belong to the Glanrafon. There were four large fields there and Mr Richards had two hundred geese on them. At sunrise I would be sent to collect the eggs before the magpies got hold of them. After that I would be sent to collect the litter off the lawns in front of the hotel, then I would wash the floors and clean the visitors' shoes and leave them outside the upstairs rooms. I would get many tips from them ... There were horses and a brake at Glanrafon to collect the visitors (*'pobol ddiarth'*) from the

station at Pwll y Frân, Traeth Coch. I would go with them with a mule and cart to bring the luggage. There were important people (*'buddigions'*) who came at that time and many of them stayed for a month. [Translated]

The coachman at the hotel was William Williams, Efail Uchaf, who was a noted 'wit' in the locality. At that time, ships' pilots would land at Moelfre and hire a 'waggonette' from the hotel, usually to be taken to the Bangor train station. One Sunday, as the car was climbing the hill near Pentraeth, one of the pilots saw sheep kneeling in the fields; they were suffering from foot-rot. The pilot called out, "Look William, what are those sheep doing on their knees?" "Well, sir," replied William Williams, "It's Sunday today. They are praying."

Games were held on the beach for the visitors and concerts held in the evenings, especially in the Glanrafon Hotel. One of the most popular events was the annual Benllech 'regatta'. John Williams, the schoolmaster, was the Secretary of the local committee, and positive reports of the occasions appeared in the newspapers:

> No watering-place worthy of the name is complete without its annual aquatic festival. Benllech, therefore, must needs have its regatta, and on Wednesday this event took place and proved a decided success. This rising place stands in an unrivalled position with magnificent scenery and a sandy beach, and it is, without doubt, destined to become one of the most important seaside resorts on the coast. Already it is favourably known to numbers of English families who annually resort thither.

Partly in response to the influx of visitors during the summer months, two new chapels were built in Benllech in the early 1900s – *Libanus* (Independent), and the *Benllech Calvinistic Methodist Chapel*. Their opening reflected the increasing popularity of the area and that the population of the village was expanding. English language services were held during the summer, and it was said that local people also attended in order to see the latest fashions on display. One Sunday, a well-known Methodist Minister from Menai Bridge lifted his head to address the congregation and exclaimed, "I thought I was looking into the display window of Wartskis!" (Wartskis was an upmarket ladies shop in Bangor).

The people who visited Benllech in the early days were generally wealthy and often brought the whole family, as well as cooks and nurses, for several weeks. Part of the attraction of the locality was that few others had discovered the beach and village, and that it remained uncommmercialised. For most people, the difficulties and expense of travelling to the area meant that the district remained inaccessible – indeed, it was said that 'more people would holiday in Benllech except that they feared that their holidays would be over by the time they arrived'.

The Railway

It was a long-held aspiration of local people to see a railway built to serve the area, yet it took over a century before the dream was fulfilled. In 1827, an Act of Parliament was passed to allow the building of a railway line from Penrhynmawr, near Gaerwen, to Red Wharf, with a view to transporting coal, lime, limestone and other products from Pentre Berw and exporting them through a dock at Red Wharf. However, nothing came of this plan. There was then a hiatus of several decades, during which time the railway line between Gaerwen, Llangefni and Amlwch was built and helped the development of Cemaes and Bull Bay as seaside locations.

From the 1880s onwards, there was mounting pressure from influential people in the district to bring a railway to the area, and several public meetings were held to promote the cause. In 1891, Lord Hussey Vivian of Plas Llanddyfnan chaired a meeting at Pentraeth to call on the London and North Western Railway (LNWR) to bring forward proposals for a railway between Llanfairpwll and Benllech. At this meeting, a letter was read out from Owen Williams, an Anglesey-born surveyor who worked for the Liverpool firm of Williams and Jones. Williams had produced the original plan for the layout of Llandudno which was adopted by the Mostyn family in the late 1840s. He had recently visited the district and sketched out a plan for the development of Benllech, and had commented that 'nature had done more towards making Red Wharf and Benllech Bay into a watering-place than she had ever done for Llandudno.' From the meeting a committee was formed to collect information and statistics of possible usage to present to the company. Again, nothing happened.

Almost five years later, another meeting in Pentraeth agreed to petition the LNWR to build a railway to Benllech. It was estimated that there were already between 1300 and 1500 visitors staying in the locality during the summer months, as well as day trippers. A railway would also be of benefit to farmers – some 500 pigs were sent from Pentraeth annually by one tradesman, as well as 6,000 tons of commodities.

Eventually, in 1897, the LNWR brought forward a proposal for a railway between Llanfairpwll and Red Wharf and Benllech. But before the necessary Act was passed, the plans were amended so that the line would branch off at Holland Arms and terminate at Pwll-y-Frân, between Benllech and Red Wharf, with a halt at Llanbedrgoch. It seems that the reason for the location of the terminus was the cost of digging a cutting through the final section, while there is also evidence that several of the landowners along the line did not support the venture and demanded high prices for land on the route. The agent for the Plas Newydd estate wrote in 1901:

> Generally I cannot see that this proposed railway is likely to benefit this Estate and certainly the price which the Railway company offer is in my opinion out of the question. The line would undoubtedly increase the value of the land at its terminus near the sea where it is intended to develop a seaside resort, but unfortunately we have no land there. I understand that the other owners have refused to entertain the offer of £40 per acre but are willing to appoint a valuer to meet the Railway Company's valuer

and to fix a price for the land severed, legislation etc and if they don't agree to leave the matter to an Umpire.

There were further delays, and at one stage it seemed unlikely that the project would go ahead. Direct representations were made to Lord Stalbridge, the chairman of the LNWR, on a visit to Bangor and he agreed to consider the case. Seven acres of the Plas Goronwy farm were bought to build the station in 1903, although work to build the track did not start until June 1907. The line to Pentraeth was opened on 1 July 1908.

Finally, on Empire Day, 24 May 1909, the first train arrived at the 'Red Wharf Bay and Benllech' station. The facilities included a booking hall and general waiting room, a booking office, a ladies waiting room and toilet, porters room, urinals, a goods shed, a small yard crane, a loading dock and a cattle pen. There was much rejoicing on the day and the assembled crowds were addressed by representatives of the LNWR and local dignitaries, including several who had worked hard to persuade the railway company over the previous twenty years:

> The Ty'nygongl postmaster, Mr. W. D. Williams, said he hoped that now the company had made a start, they would not leave Red Wharf-Benllech behind Llandudno, Colwyn Bay, Rhyl, and such places, in facilities for enabling business men to get back to business on Mondays.

Sports and a tea-party were arranged for the children of the district in the afternoon. The correspondent of *The Daily Telegraph*, who had travelled on the first train, wrote:

> The company are to be congratulated on offering their passengers a journey, without change of carriage, to the almost undiscovered joys of Anglesey, with its sparse population and picturesque rocks and heather, its sandhills strewn with sheep, and the salt winds that bring rest and health with every breath. The new route from Holland Arms to Wharf Bay and Benllech should assuredly become popular at once.

While some people locally were apprehensive of the 'commercialisation' of the area, most were very positive and saw the opportunity to link the area with the rest of North Wales – the 'playground of the British Isles'. To correspond with the opening of the line, the LNWR published postcards and a brochure highlighting the attractions of the area:

> To the Reader – This is a description of an undiscovered country for those who require a complete change ... There is a straggling irregularity about the village of Benllech which constitutes one of its principal charms.

Other commentators were similarly impressed with the district:

> The bay possesses charms for the real nature-lover that even Llandudno cannot excel. A mixture of sandhills, shingle, and rock-sloped foreshore separate the bay from an intensely characteristic Welsh village, Benllech, and between the two the sojourner who desires real unalloyed and undisturbed rest from the vexations of the known world may find them in this, which, up to the present, might have justly been the all but unknown.

> Benllech itself is unrivalled in Anglesey for what it can provide in the way of natural beauties ... beautiful as is Benllech by day, perhaps it is at its best when the evening mists are rising and obscuring the Great Orme in the far distance ... the drops of water which shimmer from the oars of the few boats which have lingered on the mirror of a sea throw off a thousand rays of phosphorescent light as they cast back the glimmering sheen of the Queen of night. But Benllech by night such as this is typical of Anglesey, and Anglesey is the pearl of North Wales.

> Until the opening last year by the LNWR of the branch line from Holland Arms, access to Benllech and Red Wharf was only obtained by a long walk or waggonette drive. Now access is comparatively easy: but the seedy man with the wheezy cornet, the barrel organ, the German

band, and the ice-cream fiend have not yet, happily, discovered the place, or, discovering it, have not found it profitable.

One local newspaper urged the railway authorities to build a pier at Benllech:

> Among North Wales resorts none has so rapidly risen in reputation as the Anglesey seaside village of Benllech ... The many steamers now plying would undoubtedly utilise any facilities for landing purposes here. "La Marguerite" lingered quite longingly in the bay the other week.

At the beginning, there were six passenger trains a day between Bangor and Red Wharf. There was also a daily goods train which carried coal, building materials, agricultural foodstuffs and animals; it was linked to a Country Lorry Service and worked from the yard on the station.

It seems that not everyone adapted overnight to the new mode of transport. Morris J. Roberts, the station master, recalled one conversation he had with a woman who asked for a ticket to Bangor, and passed him a pound note. "There's the ticket, change at Holland Arms," he said. "Oh, no, Mr Roberts," replied the lady, "I'll have my change now, thank you!"

1900 onwards

Benllech developed quickly from the turn of the century as the roads improved and different means of transport became available. The completion of the coast road around Anglesey in 1913 provided a major boost to the area, and coincided with an increase in the ownership of motor cars; it was said that the Marquis of Anglesey was a regular visitor to Benllech in his Rolls Royce.

The beach became a popular destination for day trips, with brakes running from Bangor, Beaumaris and Llangefni. Benllech was particularly popular for Sunday School outings; this was a typical report of such an excursion:

> ENGLISH BAPTIST SUNDAY SCHOOL TREAT – The members of the English Baptist Sunday School, Bangor, held their annual treat on Friday at Benllech. During the last 25 years, all the most attractive picnic resorts, accessible to Bangor, have been visited and it was after much deliberation that Benllech Bay was decided upon. At 10.30 scholars, teachers and friends assembled at the Belle Vue Hotel, where four brakes were drawn up, to carry them to Benllech. Another carriage had to be requisitioned, and then all drove off exposed to the heat of the tropical sun. Benllech was reached at one o'clock, and immediately after arrival the teachers, together with a number of friends, were invited to a hot luncheon, excellently catered for by Mrs Richards, of the Glan'rafon Hotel.
>
> The afternoon was variously spent: some sought the shady nooks, whilst others, both young and old, extracted great delight from paddling and bathing in the beautiful bay. Paddling, undoubtedly, was the order on such a broiling day. At 4.30 tea was provided for all in the spacious room attached to the hotel. The rest of the day was absorbed in games with the children and in quiet rambles along the sands and lanes. At 7.30, the bugles were blown for returning and all arrived safely in Upper Bangor at 9.30, after enjoying one of the best treats they had ever had.

The district was also popular for 'works' annual holidays. In 1910, 138 members of the Cadbury Bournville Youths Club arrived on a 'special camp train' and camped at Benllech for a week; the visit was written up in the Works Magazine. The group held daily walks to Moelfre, Beaumaris, Menai Bridge and Llangefni, played cricket against Bangor and Holyhead, and arranged sports competitions on the beach.

Scout groups visited the area regularly, and in particular the Ormskirk Troop; the Scout Master was Mr Hutton of St. Winifred's Hall near Brynteg, and proprietor of the *Ormskirk Gazette*. The Troop camped near the beach each year, and were only inconvenienced during the war years when 'owing to the military precautions the scouts will not sleep under canvas, but permission has been given to make use of the Council schools. All cooking will be done outside as usual'.

Local shopkeepers responded to the influx of visitors and took advantage of the 'golden age of postcards' from 1894 onwards when the Post Office allowed photographs and pictures to be placed on the front of postcards and addresses on the back. The first postcards of the village and beach appeared in the early 1900s when independent companies sent photographers to take pictures of local scenes. Of particular note were the studios of Mills and Wickens, both in Bangor, and Wright and Co. (W. & Co.), Bootle. It was not until later that the major companies, such as Friths and Valentines, took an interest in the district.

The area around the beach was developed further - the road down from the square was improved and the promenade was widened. Around 1910, the postmaster W. D. Williams built the Shell Café, which became a very popular meeting-place for both visitors and locals; bathing huts and deckchairs were rented out, and teas were sold on the beach. However, an inital approach to build a new road to the beach was refused, and it was not until the 1920s that the 'Bay View Road' side was built.

There was a huge demand for accommodation in the area - 'They go round begging for rooms' was a comment one summer. Adverts seeking and offering accommodation in the Manchester and Liverpool newspapers proliferated. *Bennett's Business Directory* of 1910 for Benllech Bay and Ty'n-y-Gongl advertised three of them:

> Bay View Boarding and Refreshment House and Apartments – Miss J. E. Hughes, proprietess. Two minutes' walk down to the beach. Terms moderate.

Glandŵr – Superior furnished apartments – T.E. Jones, proprietor. Every comfort and attention. Terms moderate.

Cartrefle – Mrs J. Morris Taylor. Superior furnished apartments, with board if desired. Fine sea views. Every comfort and attention.

Landowners capitalised on the development potential of their properties, and farms and smallholdings were split up into building plots in order to maximise their value. This extract for a brochure selling land at Efail Newydd and Rhosboeth in 1907 is typical of the period:

> These lots are situate close to the well-known seaside resort of Benllech Bay, and within easy reach of Red Wharf and Moelfre Bays, and are considered most suitable plots upon which to erect houses of various descriptions. The locality has become a favourite resort for summer visitors – there is an ever increasing demand for accommodation, and the construction of the new railway to Benllech should add considerably to the value of this property, the terminus being distant about a mile.

The purchasers of the land were a combination of local people with assets and others with a connection with the area. They included: John Rice Roberts, Rhiwlas, Pentraeth, solicitor and land agent; the Postmaster, W. D. Williams; Dr John Williams, Caernarfon, and previously of Tyddyn Fadog, Ty'n-y-gongl; families from Manchester and Liverpool; and retired and serving sea captains.

Perhaps the biggest change of all was to the village of Benllech itself, or 'Upper Benllech' as it was known. 'American style apartments' were built, specifically with the holiday trade in mind – Glan Aber by Tryphena Jones of Gwynfryn, and Llanddwyn House by Captain J. Thomas, who also built Nevah Wen (New Haven spelt backwards). Indeed, a local fisherman wrote to the Board of Trade to complain that a contractor was taking sand and gravel from the beach for building the new houses – the contractor agreed to stop taking the material, but pointed out that many others had been doing it for years.

A number of new shops opened along the main street, which in turn created more jobs. These included a butchers' shop (T. Pritchard and Sons, subsequently Llew Thomas), a fruit and vegetables shop (Brynydon), a grocer and bakery (Glan Aber, Margaret Williams), a draper (H. Pritchard), grocers (Môr Annedd, Mrs A Williams), and a barber's shop. Local farms and smallholdings provided eggs, butter and milk to the shops during the summer. Other services which were provided for visitors included two cab proprietors, one of whom, William Williams, Ty'nygongl Farm, was also the local undertaker and offered 'all kinds of vehicles on hire'.

New professional services were also attracted to the area, including two doctors, a 'drug store' and the London City and Midland Bank. The Bangor architect W. G. Williams opened an office in the village, and a policeman was appointed to the district - Robert Pritchard started in 1900 and a new police station was built in 1911.

A warm welcome was extended to the visitors and special concerts were laid on for them during the summer, featuring both local and outside performers. An annual ritual among the holidaymakers was the election of a 'mayor' for the village, and the following was an account of the occasion:

BENLLECH'S "MAYOR" – AN AMUSING ANGLESEY FUNCTION – On Saturday evening a large number of visitors to Benllech, the charming Anglesey seaside resort, assembled at the Glan'rafon Hotel for the purpose of carrying out the annual function established recently, *pour rire*, of electing a "mayor." "Alderman" Dunkenfield Wigward proposed the re-election of the retiring "mayor," Alderman Thomas Blackburne. "Councillor" Pryce White, representing the Bridge Ward, in seconding the proposal, said the qualifications requisite in a candidate for the "mayoralty" of Benllech Bay, were

(1) the possession of a wife worthy of the honour of being "mayoress;" (2) that the candidate should be a good "cricketer," "cricket being the staple industry of the town;" and (3) that the aspirant should be "a good fellow." All of these qualifications, he said, were in an eminent measure possessed by Alderman Blackburne. The meeting endorsed "Councillor" Pryce White's declaration with uproarious cheers, and Alderman Blackburne was unanimously re-elected.

'Bazaars' were held at the Glanrafon Hotel to raise funds for various causes; games were organised on the beach; a cricket team was formed in the village; a 9-hole golf course was opened on the Plas Gwyn fields, near Plas Thelwal, in 1911; and a bowling green was located near Beach Road.

There were, unfortunately, a number of accidents involving visitors who were unused to bathing in the sea. This report appeared in 1904:

> DROWNED AT BENLLECH – BRAVE ATTEMPT AT RESCUE – The Anglesey coroner held an inquest at Benllech, Anglesey, touching the death of Elizabeth Curtis, of 1 Schomberg-street, Liverpool, a nurse girl, seventeen years of age, engaged by Mrs Mary Birchell Barendt of 65 Rodney-street, Liverpool, who arrived at Benllech Bay on Saturday. On Sunday morning, Mrs Barendt and her sister, Miss Crowe, bathed about ten o'clock. Mrs Barendt, after being in the water some time, asked the deceased if she would like to bathe. The deceased eagerly said she would, and thereupon undressed and walked into the sea. Mrs Barendt shouted after her, but deceased apparently didn't hear, and went on and on straight out to sea. Mrs Barendt and her sister, seeing she was going too far, went after her, the latter managing to seize the deceased's hair, but failed to bring her back, as the waves were carrying the deceased out to sea. The deceased at the time gave no sign of life. Miss Crowe had to let go, and the deceased passed out to sea, the body

being subsequently recoverd by means of a boat. – The jury returned a verdict of "Accidentally drowned" and expressed their sympathy with the deceased's family, and also with Dr and Mrs Barendt. They also expressed their admiration of Miss Crowe's brave conduct in attempting to rescue the deceased.

Benllech became a popular location for wealthier families to live, especially those of sea captains who were away for several months at a time. The trend of building 'palaces' continued and others who had made money through commerce or construction in Liverpool and elsewhere also settled in the village. The houses, and their occupiers, during this period included:

Garreg Lwyd – Richard Edward Williams, retired draper

Breeze Hill – Captain Louis Roberts

Avondale – David Jones, physician and surgeon

Ivydale – William John Owen, preacher

Trefonen – Henrietta Williams, farmer and boarding house keeper

Fern Hill – Captain William Richards

Glan Adda – Captain Hugh Parry Jones

Bryn Môr – Captain Hugh Humphreys

Trosrafon/St Omer – William Jones, dispenser of medicine

Llanddwyn House – Captain John Thomas

Bryn Awel/Bryn Haul – Captain Griffith Jones

Fron Uchaf – Captain Hugh Lewis

Rhostrefor – Captain Richard John Thomas

Bryn y Wig – Captain Henry Thomas

Arwel (Ty'n-y-gongl) – Rev. John Roberts, Minister

Ty Fry (Ty'n-y-gongl) – Captain Hugh Lewis

It was also during this time that William Griffith established his building firm, and among the houses he built were:

Trem y Don/Gwynfa – Captain Richard Griffiths.

Neuadd Wen - Captain Hugh Roberts

Bryn Gwyn – Captain Hugh Williams

Argoed (Ty'n-y-gongl) - Captain Richard Williams

Visitors to Benllech continued to appreciate the beauty and tranquillity of the area, and that it had not changed a great deal since it had been 'discovered', as these two extracts from newspapers illustrate:

> Ty'nygongl Revisited – The village has not altered much in the last two years. A notable addition to the Glan'rafon shows that Mrs Richards' kindly management is attracting a wider circle of visitors than the body of pioneers who came here six or seven years ago, when wine lists were unknown and apparently not missed. There are a few new houses, and two new shops. Of these the drug store calls for remark, for here we can surely find remedies for every ailment of man or beast, with sundry extras in the way of cigars, honey, and it is rumoured hat pins. We note Moranedd also, famed for its home-made bread and its most genial bakeresses. Mrs Pritchard, too, is well settled in the shop at the corner, and even if we have nothing to buy from the excellent wealth of spades, jams, tapes, postage stamps, or Welsh stockings, we can sit at the door and look over the sunny fields and restless sea, or talk with Captain Roberts of his voyages in many seas.

On the splendid stretch of beach in Red Wharf and Benllech Bays, in the height of the holiday season, I have counted no more than 50 people. If you want to bathe you seek a secluded place among the rocks (no such things as bathing vans have ever been known there), and, undressing, plunge into the water to the accompaniment of the screaming sea gulls overhead. Inland, there are deep, cool lanes, perhaps not remarkable for the evenness of their surface, but none the worse for that, with a profusion of wild flowers growing in the hedgerows, while from every eminence there are glorious views of the Welsh mountains on the mainland.

And those who visited Benllech shared their experiences with friends and family on their postcards home:

Dear Prissy, this is a very pretty place and from the front door we can see Snowdon and see the smoke from the railway. Your loving sis Rosa.

You really ought to have been here, it is glorious. We return next year. Muriel, Glanrafon Hotel.

As you see on this postcard, this is a family resort. The sands are splendid for children, also for their pa's and ma's. We are enjoying ourselves very much.

Had a ride here [Traeth Dinas, near Traeth Bychan] yesterday. Can you pronounce it? I can't. Asked a man the way and he said he did not know the place. Pronunounced it again and he laughed outright. The Welsh are heathens.

We are having ideal weather – brilliant sunshine and the sea is perfect. We have been in the water six times. We drove in a packed brake to Llangefni on Thursday. Never had such a time in our lives.

You will wonder where this out-of-the-world place is. Well, we are in Anglesey and having a glorious time. Today we are going for a drive. With love, Ethel.

You see we have landed alright. It is very nice here but a bit too quiet. Lovely weather today. We had a rotten journey from 8.40 till 2 o'clock, it is an awful long way. Love from Mary.

Seaside holidays became popular in Britain during the pre-War period when people had more time and money to spend on leisure activities. Remoter areas such as Benllech benefitted from the improvement in roads and the increase in motorised vehicles, while the opening of the railway in 1909 gave a further boost to the district. The community responded by building more accommodation and offering more services. The locality was slowly being transformed from a distant, poor area reliant on agriculture into a more diverse and modern economy. In many ways it was a 'Golden Era' both for Benllech and the country as a whole.

17. Early visitors by Y Wig

18. At the bottom of Beach Road with John Prydderch Williams' warehouse and stores on the left

19. The road to the beach with Benllech Uchaf on the left

20. The Promenade and Sea-wall under construction, early 1900s

21. Paddling on the beach, 1909

22. Families near the second bay

23. A group enjoying the beach

24. A horse-drawn brake leaving Bangor

25. Tug of War on the beach

26. The 'Banqueting Hall' at the Cadbury Bournville Youths camp, 1910

27. The Glanrafon Hotel

28. Siop Ty'n-y-gongl in 1910, with the Post Office and one of the postmen

29. Building the railway line to Red Wharf and Benllech

30. The Red Wharf Bay and Benllech railway station, with the horse carriages waiting outside

31. The main street in the village, 1907

32. A comic postcard of the period

BENLLECH AND THE FIRST WORLD WAR

When war was declared on 4 August 1914, the Postmaster W. D. Williams was ordered to stay in the Post Office through the night in case any messages came through. Shortly after midnight the shopkeeper R. J. Lewis, a local Boer War veteran, called at the Post Office to say that a telegram was expected and it duly arrived. The following morning Roland Lloyd, the schoolmaster, asked W. D. Williams to transport a young man who had been staying with him on holiday to Menai Bridge railway station. The visitor was from Germany and his departing words were, "I hope I shall not have to fight against you."

Today, the Benllech War Memorial stands as a sombre reminder of the lives that were lost during the First World War. It records the names of nineteen men and one woman who died, and were buried, mostly in distant lands and seas far from the place they were born and lived. In 1918, some 46 men from Llanfair Mathafarn Eithaf were serving in the war, while newspaper reports indicate that at least another 25 from the area also fought at some stage. Almost one in four of the male population of the parish served during the war, and nearly two-fifths of all households in the district had at least one member who served. The conflict would have a profound effect on the community for many years afterwards.

The War Effort

The Bro Goronwy Literary Society was one of the first locally to recognise the need to provide support for those who had been displaced by the war – a collection was held In October 1914 for the Belgians who had been forced from their homes by the conflict, and one Belgian family was housed in the area. Further collections were held, and 10s was donated to provide cigarettes to serving soldiers and sailors on home leave. The first two debates of autumn 1914 at the Society were 'Is it justified for

Britain to take part in the currrent war?' (majority in favour) and 'Is a voluntary or a compulsory plan the best for creating an army?' (majority for a voluntary plan). At the end of September the Society cancelled the drama and the annual Christmas literary competition because of the war 'in the hope that there will be an early peace between the nations'. The Society itself was suspended in 1916.

Other initiatives were instigated to support the war effort. Two knitting and sewing classes were formed, one at Benllech and the other at Tabernacl; they met weekly throughout the war. Letters were read out from those who received the parcels, thanking them for the gifts and complaining bitterly that the trenches were cold and wet – 'this further motivated the sisters to sew the comforts for the men'. The older girls at Ty'n-y-gongl school knitted and sewed garments for the soldiers as part of their sewing class. In many rural districts children were encouraged to collect eggs, boil them and send them to wounded soldiers. Mrs Ellen Roger Jones, the renowned actress from Marian-glas, recounted that when she was a little girl she received a letter from a soldier recovering in a hospital in Rouen, France, to thank her for her egg, which he described as being 'very tasty' after 'rations of bully beef and hard biscuits'.

During the early stages of the war, rural areas such as Anglesey were criticised for the small numbers of young men who were volunteering to enlist. In early 1915, a local committee was established and was visited by General Owen Thomas, the lead volunteer recruiter for North Wales. In February, a military recruitment campaign was arranged on the island and 160 soldiers of the Royal Welsh Fusiliers marched through the county. When the soldiers arrived at Benllech they were addressed by the local chapel Minister and by John Rice Roberts of Rhiwlas,

> [before] sitting down to an excellent cold spread at the school ... after lunch we went to have a look at the village and sang choruses in the Square before falling in at 3.45

... Benllech gave us a hearty reception, and amongst the bunting was a banner inscribed with "Croesaw i'r Pals".

The programme continued into the evening when the troops were dined at the Glanrafon Hotel:

> The dinner was succeeded by two smoking concerts – the first party going to the Marianglas schools, and the second to Tynygongl School. Excellent programmes were provided by a number of local artistes, assisted by members of the different battalions.

The following morning the soldiers continued on their march through Rhosfawr to Llanerchymedd; they went on to Amlwch, Holyhead and Llangefni, before returning to Menai Bridge at the end of the week.

Conscription started in March 1916 and was extended to married men in May. Among those who requested exemption from service was John (Jack) Parkinson, a motor mechanic working at the Glanrafon Hotel. He stated that he was the sole support for his mother and three young children – his application was refused.

Another who applied for exemption was J. C. Parry, tailor, of Shop Tabernacl, Ty'n-y-gongl, on the grounds that he was the sole support of his mother and two sisters, and that three brothers were already in the army - his application was also refused. J. C. Parry had an eventful war. He served with the Royal Welsh Fusiliers and the Machine-Gun Corps and was wounded four times; while on leave in August 1918 he married Miss Maggie Lewis of Goronwy View, Brynteg. He was a well-known singer and choirmaster, and his choir won second place in an Eisteddfod, held at Aulnoye in France on Boxing Day after the Armistice. Following demobilisation, J. C. Parry continued his tailor's business and resumed his highly succesful career as a choirmaster.

Most of those serving from the district were Welsh-speakers. Under the title 'Lonely Soldiers', an account appeared in the *North Wales Chronicle* about Hugh Williams of Ty'n-y-gongl, and William Jones of Traeth Coch, who tried to transfer to the Welsh (Carnarvonshire) Royal Garrison Artillery because there were no Welsh-speakers with them at their battalions. The Bangor magistrates requested the military authorities to transfer them to regiments where Welsh was spoken.

A handful of regular soldiers were stationed at Benllech to protect the coastline from foreign invasion. The author Siân Williams, who was brought up at Refail Uchaf, Ty'n-y-gongl, described in her autobiography that one of them, an Irishman nicknamed Paddy, challenged Siân and her friend as they crossed the beach one day, *"Halt, who goes there? Friend or Foe? If it wasn't for me you would be seeing Kaiser Bill and his battalions over there and there and there."* It seems that the girls took little notice of the protection being offered to them.

At the beginning of 1917, a meeting was called to establish a detachment of the Anglesey Volunteer Force – the 'Tynygongl Platoon'. The platoon was commanded by Lieutenant R. J. Lewis, Siop Ty'n-y-Gongl, who was 'formerly in the Army and saw active service in the South African war'. The Company trained twice a week and provided guards for duty on the Tubular Bridge at Menai Bridge.

The Defence of the Realm Act was introduced in 1914 and added to as the war progressed. It brought in restrictions on various activities, and several local individuals fell foul of the law:

> William Jones of Traeth Coch was found guilty of failing to obscure a light in one of the windows of his house and fined 5s.. Lights were not meant to be visible to the enemy at sea.

> Thomas Williams of Tyddyn Fadog was charged with selling adulterated (watered down) milk. He maintained in court that this was because the cows had been fed with

straw because his supply of hay had run out. The court did not believe his explanation and he was fined £5.

John Thomas, the landlord of the California Inn, Brynteg, was charged with selling a bottle of stout after 8pm and with accepting an order for spirits after 2.30pm; Ellen Jones of Gloddfa Bach, Llaneugrad, was charged with purchasing the alcohol. The cases against Ellen Jones were dismissed with a caution, while John Thomas was fined 10s and the special constable's fee of 5s for selling spirits after 2.30 pm.

Hugh William Richards, licencee of the Glanrafon Hotel, was fined £10 for employing a soldier named Robert Thomas, knowing him to be a deserter. 'The defendant said Thomas had told him he would go back when he was fetched, and rather than see the man idling about he gave him some work to do.' This may have prompted him to be more careful when he advertised for a chauffeur later during the war: 'Wanted, immediately, good, steady Chauffeur; able to do repairs; discharged Soldier or one ineligible for the Army'.

The Fallen

While there may have been an air of normality in the daily life of many in the community, the situation was very different for those individuals and families directly involved in the conflict. Several local men enlisted voluntarily as soon as war was declared, and it was not long before news reached home of the deaths and injuries suffered by those involved in the conflict. Memorial services for the fallen were held regularly in the local chapels and churches.

The whole district was rocked to its core when, on 6th June 1915, the *SS Gertrude*, a coastal steamer carrying a load of coal from Ellesmere Port to Waterford in Ireland, collided with the troopship *SS City of Vienna* in dense fog. The *SS Gertrude* sank and only one of the crew of nine survived. Five of the crew members who died were from the Llanallgo and Moelfre area, including **John Owen**, mate, who lived with his wife Kate and six children at Strand View, Benllech, before the war.

In September 1917 it was reported that:

> Many families in the neighbourhood have suffered losses during the past week, the war having exacted a heavy toll on your young men, particularly at sea ... This sequence of bad news has cast a gloom over the district.

Six men had been killed or were missing during that week. A further three men from the area were killed in a single incident a matter of weeks later.

A brief description of those who were killed and who are recorded on the Benllech War Memorial is as follows.

Private Edward G Evans, Tan Dinas, Brynteg - Edward Evans was the eldest son of Richard and Ann Evans, Tan Dinas, and served with the 1st Battalion, Royal Welsh Fusiliers. He was killed in action on the Western Front on 12 January 1917, and is buried at the Serre Road Cemetery, Somme, France. Memorial services were held for him both at the Llanfair M. E. Parish Church and the Baptist Chapel, where he was a member, and where 'high tributes were paid to his character and self-sacrifice'.

Private Robert W Evans, Waen, Bwlchgwyn - Robert Evans was the eldest son of John and Elizabeth Evans, Waen, Bwlchgwyn. He and his brother Humphrey enlisted voluntarily at the outbreak of the war - both were working as coal miners in South Wales at the time. Robert served with the 11th Battalion, Royal Welsh Fusiliers and was killed in action on 28 June 1918 in Salonika, Greece, aged 31. He is buried at the Karasouli Military Cemetery, Greece.

Private Humphrey Evans, Waen, Bwlchgwyn – Humphrey Evans was the second brother to be killed, and served with the

1/5th Battalion, East Lancashire Regiment. He died in France on 14 November 1918 due to the effects of poison gas and pneumonia, aged 28, and is buried at the Etaples Military Cemetery, Pas de Calais, France. The youngest brother, Gunner John Evans, served with the Royal Field Artillery; he was reported to be suffering from shellshock in 1917, but survived the war.

Jane Ellen Howdle, Pantysaer, Tynygongl – Jane Howdle is the only woman commemorated on the Benllech War Memorial. She was the daughter of Mr and Mrs John Hughes, Pant y Saer Uchaf, Ty'n-y-gongl, and the widow of Benjamin Howdle. She was a stewardess on board the passenger ship Lusitania, which was sunk by the German submarine *U-20* on 7 May 1915 – one of thirteen out of 22 stewardesses on board who perished. She was aged 33 and left three children, at least one of whom was subsequently brought up at Pant y Saer. Jane Ellen Howdle is buried at the Cobh Old Church Cemetery, Cobh, County Cork, Ireland. The sinking of the Lusitania was one of the worst single atrocities of the First World War with the loss of 1,191 lives.

Captain Henry William Hughes, Brynhyfryd, Tynygongl - Henry William Hughes was the son of Elizabeth and the late Captain Thomas Hughes, of Brynhyfryd, Ty'n-y-gongl, and was living at the Post Office, Trefor, Llanaelhaiarn. He was First Mate on the *SS Cymrian*, a cargo steamer which was torpedoed and sunk on 25 August 1917 in the St Georges Channel by the German submarine *UC-75* when on route for Dublin with a cargo of coal. 10 crew members were lost, including his nephew John Rowlands. Henry William Hughes was 48 years old.

Private Edward Owen, Pen yr Odyn, Rhos Fawr - Edward Owen was one of five brothers who fought in the war. They were the sons of John and Catherine Owen of Pen yr Odyn, Rhos Fawr. Edward enlisted voluntarily early in the war; he was working as a ploughman and was living at home. He served with the 11th Battalion, Royal Welsh Fusiliers and was initally posted to France; his unit was then moved to the Macedonian front. He died of malaria on 16 December 1917 in Salonika, Greece, aged

25, and is buried at the Salonika (Lembet Road) Military Cemetery, Thessalonika, Greece.

Private William Owen, Pen yr Odyn, Rhos Fawr - William Owen was the second brother of the Pen yr Odyn family to be killed. Prior to enlisting he worked for Great Western Railway in Llanelli. William served with the 7th Battalion, South Wales Borderers; he also died at Salonika, killed in action, aged 27 years old, on 5 February 1919. He is buried in the Tiflis (now Tiblisi) Cemetery, Georgia, and is now commemorated officially in Istanbul. Three other Pen yr Odyn brothers also fought in the War – Owen, Morris, and Joseph. Joseph was severely wounded during the war and discharged.

Private William Richard Owen, Fron Uchaf - William Richard Owen was the only surviving son of Mrs Elizabeth Owen, 2 Fron Deg, and served with the 1/6th Battalion Royal Welsh Fusiliers. Prior to joining the army he was working as a baker and vanman at Y Fron, Benllech. He died of fever in Egypt on 2 March 1917 and is buried at the Kantara War Memorial Cemetery, Egypt.

Gunner Willie Owen, Ty Newydd, Benllech – William (Willie) Owen was the only son of Captain Moses and Mrs Mary Owen, Tŷ Newydd, and served with the 22nd Brigade, Royal Field Artillery. He was seriously wounded at the Battle of Passchendale on 31 October 1917 and taken to the Australian General Hospital, Wimereux. His parents travelled to see him at one of the base hospitals the following month. He was thought to be recovering well before suddenly deteriorating and died on 22 December 1917 before his parents could be summoned to see him again. He is buried at the Wimereux Communal Cemetery, Pas de Calais, France. Signaller Owen was 19 years old and was preparing for the teaching profession when he joined the army. He was described as 'a young man of sterling character'.

Private Michael Roberts, Pendref, Cefniwrch – Michael Roberts served with the 14th Battalion, Royal Welsh Fusiliers. He died of pneumonia at Alresford, Winchester, where his unit was training nearby, on 18 November 1915. He was aged 27 and is buried at Capel Soar, Brynteg.

Private Rhys Roberts, Bryn Celyn, Benllech – Rhys Roberts served with the 17th Battalion, The King's (Liverpool) Regiment. He and two others were accidentally killed in the Somme, France, by the premature explosion of a grenade which he was priming, on 14 January 1916, aged 24. He is buried at the Cerisy-Gailly Cemetery, Somme, France. Rhys Roberts was originally from Nant Gwynant, Caernarfonshire, and had lived in Liverpool for five years, working as a cotton porter. Two of his brothers were also killed in the war. The previous year he had married Edith Mary Griffiths who lived at Bryn Celyn, Benllech – a son, also called Rhys, was born a month after his father's death.

Private William Roberts, Bron Felen, Cefniwrch – William Roberts was the son of William and Elizabeth Roberts, Bron Felen, and served with the 17th Battalion, Royal Welsh Fusiliers. He was killed during the 2nd Battle of Bapaume, France, on 3 September 1918, aged 21, and is buried at the Sailly-Saillisel British Cemetery. It was initally reported that he had been wounded and was in hospital; he was then reported as missing and his parents did not receive official notification that he had been killed until May 1919. His brother John Roberts also served.

Private Jack (John Owen) Thomas, Llanddwyn, Benllech - Jack Thomas was the son of Captain J. and Mrs Thomas of Llanddwyn House, Benllech. He joined the 2nd West Lancashire Field Ambulance, Royal Army Medical Corps, in September 1914 and suffered gassing during his active service in France. Following his medical discharge he had been in 'indifferent health' and he died in Bangor Military Hospital on 22 August 1919, aged 30. He is buried at the Llanfair Mathafarn Eithaf parish churchyard. His brother Joseph Henry Thomas also served in the R.A.M.C..

Private David Williams, Pantybugail, Tynygongl – David Williams was a farm labourer and the son of Owen and Elizabeth Williams, Pantybugail. He served with the 9th Battalion, Royal Welsh Fusiliers, and was initally wounded at Pilken Ridge on 31 July 1917. He was reported missing, believed killed in action, at the Battle of the Lys, France between 8 and 18 April 1918, aged 28. He is commemorated on the Tyne Cot Memorial, Zonnebeke, Belgium.

Private Hugh Henry Williams, Tudno View, Benllech – Hugh Henry Williams was the son of Richard and Elizabeth Williams, Tudno View, the youngest of eight sons, and served with the 72nd Canadian Infantry. He moved to Canada at the outbreak of war, and was working as a clerk when he enlisted. He was killed in action in the Battle of Arras, France, on 9 April 1917, aged 22. He is commemorated on the Vimy Memorial, France.

Lieutenant John Richard Williams, Ynysfor, Benllech - John Richard Williams was the son of Griffith and Catherine Williams, Ynysfor. He was a Volunteer Reserve who served in the Royal Navy on *HMMS Blackmorevale*, a minesweeper. He was killed when his ship struck a mine off Montrose, Scotland, on 1 May 1918, aged 23; 26 crew members were lost from a complement of 73. His younger brother, Griffith Williams, in the merchant navy, had a 'very narrow escape' when his ship was torpedoed and he spent many hours in the water.

Second Lieutenant Lewis R Williams, Gwynfryn, Benllech - Lewis R Williams was the son of John Williams, the headmaster of Ty'n-y-gongl Board School, and Tryphena, the daughter of Lewis Roberts, Siop y Fron. He was working in a bank in Warwick and volunteered when war broke out. He served in the 10th Battalion, Royal Welsh Fusiliers and was killed in action during the Battle of the Somme on 18 August 1916, aged 22. He is commemorated on the Thiepval Memorial, Somme, France, and a memorial plaque to him was placed in the Benllech C.M. chapel.

Driver Owen Williams, Gwynfryn - Owen Williams was the second of the Williams brothers to be killed and served with the 2/1st Battery Warwickshire Royal Household Artillery. He entered a drapery business in Dublin and later lived in London and Rouen, France, where he served as an interpreter during the early stages of the war. He died of his wounds during the Third Battle of Ypres on 30 September 1917, aged 31. He is buried at the Dozinghem Military Cemetery, Westvleteren, Belgium. A memorial service was held at the Benllech Congregational Chapel in November 1918 where a mural tablet was unveiled by his brother, Driver Hugh Morris Williams; the testimony of Owen Williams' officer was read out at the service where it was stated that 'he sacrificed his life to save his comrades'. His brother John Ivor Williams, and step-brother William Jones, also served during the war.

Private Owen Williams, Glanrafon Bach, Benllech - Owen Williams was married to Lucy Mary Williams, Glanrafon Bach. He served with the 13th Battalion, Royal Welsh Fusiliers and was living in Manchester when he enlisted. He died of his wounds on 28 August 1916 at the Casualty Clearing Station, near Poperinghe, Belgium, aged 35, and is buried at the Lijssenthoek Military Cemetery, Poperinghe, Belgium.

Able Seaman William Williams, Sport y Gwynt - William Williams was the son of Robert and Catherine Williams, Sport y Gwynt, and was lodging at Seacombe, Cheshire. He was a crew member of the *S.S. Dotterel* which was sailing from Manchester to Dunkirk with general cargo when it was sunk on 29 November 1915 by a German mine off Boulogne, France. Aged 32, he was one of five lives lost.

As can be seen from the brief descriptions above, the deaths represented a whole swathe of the community - a ploughman, a railway worker, two miners, a farm labourer, a baker, two bank workers, a cotton porter, a clerk, a trainee teacher and a stewardess. In a closely-knit rural district such as Benllech, with close family ties, the impact of the deaths would have been felt acutely in the chapels and the church, the school, and the shops in the village.

Other families in the area also had traumatic experiences. **Corporal Thomas Roberts** was the youngest son of Thomas and Ann Roberts, Tŷ Mawr, Llanfair Mathafarn Eithaf, and served with the 10th Battalion, Royal Welsh Fusiliers. Prior to enlisting, he was Assistant Master at Ty'n-y-gongl school, and was attending a teaching course at Bangor Normal College. He has killed on 13 November 1916 at the Battle of Ancre, the final engagement of the Battle of the Somme. He was recorded as 'wounded missing' and his parents contacted the International Red Cross Society asking for any information on Thomas. Due to an unfortunate mix up with another soldier with a similar name, they were initially told that he was a prisoner of war, only for that to be corrected later. The family was not told formally that he was presumed dead until December 1917. He was aged 24 and is commemorated at the Thiepval Memorial, France, and the Marian-glas War Memorial.

Thomas Roberts' elder brother, Robert John (Bob) enlisted with the 21st Battalion, Manchester Regiment, but shortly afterwards 'deserted' from the army and disappeared. Several years later he re-appeared in Anglesey in a dishevelled state and mentally damaged; following enquiries, he was re-united with his parents and lived with them afterwards.

Some soldiers from the district were taken prisoner or injured during the conflict. **Lieutenant Rev. Idwal B. Roberts**, was the Minister of the Benllech C. M. Chapel from 1911 until 1914 when he enlisted as a chaplain in the British Expeditionary Force. He resigned that post in order to serve 'in the firing line' and was hospitalised in France in 1918, having had his right arm amputated, and was also reported to be suffering from a thigh wound.

Among those who served from the locality were **Captain Hugh Roberts**, Neuadd Wen, Benllech. He was an experienced master mariner and was commissioned as a Lieutenant of the Inland

Water Transport, Royal Engineers. He served in Mesopotamia (Iraq) before being posted to military headquarters. After the war he resumed his illustrious career in the merchant navy, before retiring to Benllech.

Many of those who were killed are buried or commemorated in far-away countries, while others were lost at sea. Perhaps the most poignant memorials are those on the gravestones of the Evans brothers of Waen, Bwlch, and of John Richard Williams, Ynysfor, respectively, at the Tabernacl cemetery:

"Byw bob dydd lle mynno'i hun/ A marw lle mynno Duw"

[Translated: "Live each day wherever one wishes/And die where God wills"]

"O! Y fynwent heb feini!/ Tywyll, oer, fynwent y lli"

[Translated: "Oh! The cemetery without tombstones!/ Dark, cold, the grave of the sea"]

The Aftermath

The end of hostilities on 11 November 1918 was greeted with great joy in the area - 'Bunting was displayed and a special thanksgiving service was held at the Benllech C. M. chapel' – though many servicemen continued to fight in the arenas of war. United services were held in the chapels of the district, while gifts were collected for those who remained on active service. Later, suppers, concerts and a sports day were arranged and attended by demobilised sailors and soldiers.

The celebrations were more muted than they might have been as the area was in the grip of an influenza epidemic. Several children and young people died during the outbreak, including sisters Jennie (17) and Katie Williams (19), the daughters of Captain and Mrs Huw Williams, Bryn Gwyn, Benllech; Captain Williams was unable to arrive in time from his ship for the funeral of his youngest daughter. The epidemic continued into the following year.

The North Wales Heroes Memorial Appeal was launched in 1917; Lord Boston was appointed President of the Ty'n-y-gongl district committee and promised £250 towards the fund. The Ty'n-y-gongl area was one of the most successful in Anglesey for raising monies, with numerous concerts held and organisations such as the Literary Society playing a full part in the fundraising. In 1919 a 'peace celebration committee' was established to provide a gift to those who were still serving overseas.

Thoughts also turned to the need to establish a suitable memorial in the village for those who had lost their lives, although it seems as though there was some tension as to what would be the most appropriate form of remembrance. It had long been an aspiration of the Literary Society and others to build a village hall with a library; despite several attempts, this had not been fulfilled. The parish council revived the idea in 1919 and proposed a hall to commemorate both the poet Goronwy Owen and those fallen in WW1. A site was identified with the co-operation of Lord Boston, and fundraising began. At the same time, there was also a 'Benllech Committee' which was also collecting donations for a memorial.

In the event, the Benllech War Memorial was the first to be erected on the square and was unveiled on 4 August 1922 by Mrs Megan Lloyd George, the daughter of David Lloyd George, the war-time Prime Minister, and by Brigadier-General Sir Owen Thomas M.P.. The event was reported in the Holyhead Chronicle:

> Benllech's Fallen Heroes – Memorial Unveiled. On Friday, Mrs Lloyd George unveiled a roadside war memorial to the fallen heroes of the parish of Llanfair Mathafarn Eithaf. A large number of residents and visitors assembled, the Rev. D. J. Davies, curate, presiding over the ceremony. The Revs. H. R. Cadwaladr, R. R. Jones,

W. Price and Oliver Harding (rector) took part. The singing was led by Mr J. Charles Parry and Miss Jones, Fferam, gave an impressive rendering of *"Gyda'r Wawr"*.

Mrs Lloyd George spoke feelingly in Welsh and English, and Sir Owen Thomas, M.P., Mr S. J. Evans M.A. [Headmaster of the Llangefni County School] and Mr R. Lloyd (Council School) also spoke. Master Lionel Jones, a member of the Llangefni Town Band, sounded the "Last Post" and buglers of the Ormskirk Scouts, which are camping in the neighbourhood, in charge of Mr Hutton, jnr, were also present at the ceremony. The memorial is of local limestone partially dressed with a marble slab.

The site was presented by Capt. Warren Evans, J.P., Henblas, and Mrs Richards, Glanrafon Hotel, collected most of the money towards the memorial, Mrs Jones, Gwynfryn, and the Rev. D. J. Davies acting as secretaries.

33. Private J. C. Parry, dressed in the uniform of the Argyll and Sutherland Highlanders

34. Private Edward Owen, Pen yr Odyn, Rhos Fawr, one of five brothers who fought in the War

35. Driver Owen Williams, Gwynfryn, Benllech, whose brother was also killed during the War

36. Captain Hugh Roberts, Neuadd Wen, Benllech

37. The unveiling of the Benllech War Memorial, 1922, with Brigadier-General Sir Owen Thomas M.P.

38. The crowd at the unveiling, with Gwynfryn and Siop y Fron in the background

A WELL ESTABLISHED SEASIDE RESORT

Despite the continued loss of British lives in Europe, seaside resorts in the UK continued to prosper during the war years and Benllech was no exception. In summer 1914 the holiday season was in full swing, concerts and eisteddfodau were being held, and the chapels and church were running their weekly services. Yet some, at least, were aware of the emerging conflict. In August 1914 the Red Wharf Bay and District Horticultural Society held its Annual Show at the Glanrafon Hotel where 'more than expected attended despite the call to arms'.

Holidaymakers and day-trippers continued to visit the area in droves. In summer 1916, a family from Llandudno were staying at Bay View and sent a series of postcards of the village to their son, Gunner Edgar Bruce Evans, who was training at the Fulwood Training Camp, Preston, with the Royal Field Artillery – 'We are all disappointed you're not coming here, you must come on your next leave'. Gunner Evans served for over two years more until the end of the war and afterwards went back to Llandudno to resume his career as an upholsterer; it is not known whether he did visit Benllech.

In the summer of 1917 it was reported that:

> Every available house in the district is now occupied by visitors, and all the usual pastimes are indulged in to the full – bathing, boating, fishing, golfing, etc ... Visitors and residents are pleased to have the company of Mr F G Blackburne once more, after an absence of a few seasons. He was always recognised as the "Mayor" of Benllech during his stay. Mr Blackburne captained the very strong cricket team which the Benllech visitors generally sent to play Bangor and other clubs in pre-war days.

In August 1918 it was stated that:

> In addition to the unprecedented number of visitors staying at the Benllech and Red Wharf district, a host of day trippers came here on Monday, and the beach presented a very animated appearance all day.

The Ormskirk Boy Scouts were again camping in the area and 'beat a scratch team of the local Volunteers by 108 points to 80' at the Mathafarn Rifle Range. At the end of the season a special train was run from the Red Wharf and Benllech Station to carry the departing visitors and 'a record September is promised'.

Local fishermen were busy during the summer months providing a regular supply of fish to visitors and residents, and good hauls of herring were lifted from the Moelfre area. There was a shortage of labour as more agricultural labourers were enlisted; schools were closed to enable children to assist farmers, and soldiers on leave were sent to the district to help with harvesting. A Private Dyson, employed for some months doing farmwork at Tudor Villa, had 'become very popular in the neighbourhood' and his departure for Valley was 'regretted by many'.

A changing community

Although the inter-war period was a time of depression and unemployment in Britain, living standards rose for most people. Seaside resorts benefitted from the reduction in the working week and the spread of paid holidays, while the rapid expansion in the number of private motor cars, and the greater use of buses, meant that even remote places like Benllech were within easy access of the major urban centres.

After the war ended, the societies and clubs which had been suspended were re-established. In November 1919, the Bro Goronwy Literary Society met for the first time in three years; over 100 members joined and it was decided to revive the annual Christmas competition. Although the Society essentially continued in the same format as in earlier years, there started to be changes which perhaps reflected wider developments within society. The Society took on the mantle of appointing a 'Mayor' for the district, which had previously been the preserve of the 'visitors'. They also held 'whist drives' to raise funds, which would have been inconceivable during the early years of the Society.

Another change which reflected the growing interest in sporting activities during the era was the creation of the Benllech football team. The club was started in 1920 with local men, but in 1922 others came to play and the team included players from Llangefni, Bangor and Caernarfon. The club colours were blue and white stripes, and the ground was a field on Fferam – one goal had its back to the Glanrafon Hotel and there was a slope towards the river. Mrs Richards, the proprietess of the Hotel, was the club President.

The Benllech team had its major success during the 1922/23 season when they reached the final of the inaugural Dargie Cup, the Anglesey League knock-out competition. The game was played on the old Bangor City ground, and the opponents were a strong Llandegfan team. The score was 1-1 at half time, with Ifor Jones from Bethesda scoring the winning goal in the second half. Benllech were the first winners of the trophy, and the competition still exists today. It seems that the fortunes of the Benllech team fell away after the final and they were never as succesful afterwards.

Tennis courts were built in the village and the golf course, which was closed during the war, was reconstructed and reopened in the early 1920s. It had its own professional and greenkeeper; in the mid 1930s visitors' fees were 2s 6d a day, 10s a week and 15s 6d a fortnight. Sunday play was allowed. The golf club was wound up following World War 2.

Alongside these new leisure activities, the more traditional side of the community continued to flourish. The chapels and church were their usual hive of activity; large numbers of the population continued to attend, though they were perhaps no longer the focal points of the community as they had been in the past.

The Ty'n-y-gongl School also thrived, albeit that the numbers at the school were lower than at the beginning of the century. Challenges remained in terms of attendance:

> 24 July 1931 - The attendance of late has been rather low, the boys being kept away to assist with the hay harvest when the weather permits work. Some of the girls also help at home with visitors.

Illnesses continued to affect the area and in March 1933 the school was closed for three weeks because of a measles epidemic. An unusual incident with a snake the following year caused excitement, as noted in the school logbook:

> 25 April 1934 - Two of the upper class boys killed a viper near Pen-y-bonc and brought it to school. It measured twenty-one inches. A lesson was given on "The Common Viper" to the upper class.

Another traditional activity in the community was the choir, and one choir in particular enjoyed remarkable success from the 1920s onwards. Côr Bro Goronwy was led by John Charles (J. C.) Parry, war-veteran, as choirmaster. Over the years the choir won three first prizes, one second and one fourth prize at the National Eisteddfod, and won prizes in many other Eisteddfodau. J. C. Parry led a number of other choirs and was choirmaster of Côr Bro Goronwy for over 60 years. Another choir from the district was Côr Mathafarn – they also won the competition at the National Eisteddfod, and were awarded a special shield by Lady Megan Lloyd George for winning the Anglesey Eisteddfod three times during the 1930s.

There were also significant changes to the infrastructure in the village during the inter-war period. In 1919 it was stated that:

Notwithstanding the general scarcity of water during the drought there has been no lack of water at Benllech this year, a new well having been connected with the supply. After boring about four yards a new spring of excellent water has been tapped near Ty'nygongl School. It may interest many to know that Mr Richard Owen, the Llanerchymedd water diviner, located this spring.

During the 1920s and 1930s, the local springs would be gradually replaced by a small reservoir in the centre of the village, and a mains supply would come to the district. The area was also connected to the electricity network in the late 1930s, although it would be many years before some of the outlying houses and farms were linked up.

The shooting of Constable Robert Pritchard

One event would shock the whole locality – the shooting of Constable Robert Pritchard in 1924. Robert Pritchard was born in 1874 in Tyddyn Engan, Penysarn; he was one of eight children. In 1899 he joined the Anglesey Constabulary and was stationed at Holyhead, Ty'n-y-gongl, Newborough, Brynsiencyn and Gwalchmai. He was very popular locally and served at Ty'n-y-gongl between 1900 and 1908. During his time in the village he lived at Cae Merddyn and married Ann Jones, from nearby Minffordd farm; they had nine children.

On 21st November 1924, Hugh Thomas Owen, a land agent from Llangefni, went to a farm at Cemaes Newydd, Gwalchmai, to collect overdue rent of £27. The 60-year old tenant, John Davies, told Mr Owen to 'go back to the road or I'll shoot you' and brandished a double-barrelled shotgun. It appeared that there had been a family dispute and John Davies had been served notice to quit by his cousin. The land agent retreated and went to fetch the local policeman, P.C. Robert Pritchard, from Gwalchmai. Both men went to the farm and, after speaking with the tenant's wife, Constable Pritchard went up the stairs. He was shot in the chest and was taken by car to the Caernarvon and Anglesey hospital in Bangor, where he died from his injuries the following day. Following the shooting, a cordon of the Anglesey Constabulary surrounded the farmhouse and kept it under observation through the night. About 11.00 am a little girl came out and told the police that her father was in bed. The police then entered the house and arrested Davies. He was taken to Holyhead police station initially and two months later he was convicted and jailed for seven years for manslaughter.

Following a service at the hospital, Constable Pritchard's body was transported to Tabernacl Chapel, Ty'n-y-gongl, with his helmet and truncheon resting on his coffin. A service was held at the chapel, led by the Rev. Theophilius Lewis and Chief Constable Robert Humphrey Protheroe, and he was interred at the Tabernacl Cemetery. Two of Constable Pritchard's daughters were working in Crewe at the time, and found out about the shooting of their father on a newsstand.

A memorial to Constable Robert Pritchard was unveiled at the Police Headquarters, Colwyn Bay, in 1985, and he is commemorated on the National Police Memorial in central London.

The seaside resort

Holidaymakers continued to flock to the area and, by all accounts, 1919 was a bumper year as the following reports from the *North Wales Chronicle* illustrate:

> April – 'An unusually large number of visitors spent the Easter holidays at Benllech and Red Wharf Bay'.
>
> June – 'Benllech and Red Wharf Bay had an unprecedented number of visitors for the Whitsuntide hiolidays. Most of the houses are already occupied, or likely to be so, before the end of the month. Many applications for July and August have been refused. The beach was invaded on Monday by a host of trippers from the countryside, who, favoured by ideal weather, greatly enjoyed themselves'.

August – 'In common with all seaside resorts the Benllech and Red Wharf district is crowded with visitors, many having perforce to take accommodation in the outlying farmhouses. As usual, the entertainments at the Glan'rafon Assembly Room are well patronised. Fancy dress balls and dances are also frequently held'.

Later in the year, the herring season got underway:

No big catches are yet reported. It is at times like these that the want of a jetty is keenly felt, and it is hoped that the County Council will be able to prevail upon the Fisheries' Commissioners to erect one here without much more delay.

There was plenty of entertainment for the visitors during the summer months, and the Glanrafon Hotel and Ballroom became the main centre for concerts and dances. A garage opened alongside the hotel which was initially managed by John (Jack) Parkinson, and later by O. Glyn Parry. The hotel attracted an ecletic group of entertainers. The following advert appeared in 'The Stage' in 1924:

WANTED, Really Good Resp. Gent. with turn. Refined, cap. line. Resps. with turns write in. Dress well on and off. Money sure. – DOROTHY LA'VANT, Glanrafon Hotel, Benllech Bay, Tyn-y-Gongl, Anglesey.

In the early 1920s there were further developments around the beach. The Promenade was widened to allow access for cars, and they parked on the sand-dunes at the end of the road. The site was further modified when William Griffith and his son Emrys bought the land behind the beach in 1929; they used the sand for building houses in the district and also sold the material as *Tywod Benllech* (Benllech sand) which became well-known on the island. Indeed, when the local supply ran out, sand from Penrhoslligwy, Rhosneigr and Treaddur was also sold as *Tywod Benllech*. In the 1940s, the firm carried sand from the area to the new Butlins camp at Pwllheli.

When the sand was removed, it left a flat area and the Griffiths built the Wendon Café there around 1930. It became a very popular destination, with twenty staff and two chefs employed at one stage. The land around the café was later bought by the Anglesey County Council and it became the car park for the beach.

The area behind the cliffs also became popular as a picnicing site; it was known as 'Happy Valley'. Wooden beach huts were built there, and these were extended to the 'second bay'.

Many visitors continued to arrive by train at the Red Wharf Bay and Benllech railway station . Morris J. Roberts, the stationmaster between 1921 and 1930, said:

> It was particularly busy at weekends during the holiday seasons, and it is recalled that on Saturday afternoons, to meet the train due at 4.00pm there would be anything between 45 and 50 vehicles, traps, carts, but at that time only very few motor cars ... there would be some 300 passengers, mostly visitors for a large area.

The railway also served a useful function when there was a glut of herrings. Morris Roberts recalled a particularly busy season:

> During the winter of 1922/23 there was a very exceptional influx of fish (herrings only) in the bays – Benllech, Traeth Bychan and Moelfre. This meant a transport problem which only the railway could, and did, solve to the large English cities. It is recorded that during this particular season, in a fortnight, 500 tons of herrings were loaded in 12 special trains, each comprising 8 to 12 vans for distribution to such places as London, Liverpool, Manchester, Birmigham etc.

A further record haul occured in the autumn of 1928 when over 3,000 barrels and boxes of herring were transported in one fortnight period on special overnight trains to the main markets.

However, the train service was facing increased competition from the growth in private car ownership and the introduction of motorised buses. The Automobile Association listed the picnic site near the seashore as being a site which they had checked was safe to park cars without the risk of incoming tides! In the late 1920s, bus services known as the Bangor Blue and the Mona Maroon were started from Bangor and Llangefni, and these became very popular. A return ticket to Bangor on the train cost 1s 11d while the bus cost 2s 3d. Most people chose the bus because of the convenience.

Regular railway passenger services to Red Wharf and Benllech stopped in 1930. Passenger trains were still run on Saturdays during the summer months until 1939 because the buses could not cope with the volume of tourist traffic to and from Benllech (there were restrictions on the size and weight of buses crossing the Menai Bridge until the 1940s). The line continued as a goods service, but even this dwindled and the railway closed to all traffic in 1950. In retrospect, it seems that the railway service to Benllech was marginal from the outset, while the change at Holland Arms and the location of the station lengthened journeys and made them more inconvenient. After the huge effort that was made to open a railway station, it closed to regular passenger trains barely twenty years from its opening.

Modern Benllech emerges

A number of property sales took place after the war which would alter the size and shape of the village. By this time, the land agents and auctioneers were well aware of the tourist potential of Benllech, and the attractiveness of the locations were highlighted in the advertising material:

> 1918 – Penycoed House and farm – 22 acres. 'This forms a nice building estate ripe for development. It is situate on a bold headland overlooking the Irish Sea, between the far-famed Red Wharf Bay and Benllech Bay, both places now well established as favourite seaside summer resorts, and where there is an increasing demand for accommodation

every year. The bathing here is good, and the sea fishing is excellent. The Red Wharf Bay and Benllech Railway Station is within a short distance'.

1919 – Sixteen building sites along the main coastal road near Mynachlog and Efail Newydd. 'This well-placed and very desirable building land occupies an exceptionally good position overlooking and within easy reach of the popular and growing seaside resort of Benllech. It is skirted by the Main Coastal Road leading from Menai Bridge to Amlwch, and the London and North Western Railway Station brings the property into direct communication with the great industrial centres of Lancashire, Cheshire and the Midlands. The land has good road frontages, and owing to its slightly elevated position commands beautiful uniterrupted views of the Great Orme, Puffin Island, the Irish Sea, and practically the whole of the Snowdonian Range, and forms ideal sites for the erection of bungalows or larger residences on this portion of the beautiful coastline'.

The most important sale during this period was the 1922 auction of 33 acres of land which was formerly part of Fferam, and which later became known as Bay View Road. The estate was being sold by Alleyne Evan Edward Blennerhassett Williams, of Craig Ard, Benllech, who had inherited it from his father Dr Evan Williams of Greenhill, Llangefni. The land was divided into 55 lots, which extended to the beach, and the plan showed a proposed road which would link up with the Promenade.

A special brochure was produced for the sale, which boasted:

The tendency of the discriminating section of the public is to seek recreation and change of scene at the less frequented resorts along the bold and picturesque coast of Anglesey, which, retaining their rural charm, have all the natural advantages of the more "fashionable" watering-places. Benllech is easily in the forefront in this respect. The climate is bracing, sea bathing excellent, and the extensive sands are safe an unsurpassed for children's enjoyment. Fishing and sailing form a great attraction, and there is full scope both for deep sea and hand-line fishermen, and lobsters are plentiful.

The property, in the form of a natural ampitheatre, slopes gently seaward directly to the shore, to which it has good frontage including what will in time form the Marine Parade. The situation is unique. No other building operations on adjacent land can interfere with the amenities of this property. It commands extensive and uniterrrupted views of the Irish Sea and Welsh Mountains.

The present sale provides an exceptional opportunity not only for the far-sighted investor who, realizing the possibilities of the development of this district, buys with the certainty of an early and substantial return for his money, but also for those who desire to have as their own a modest bungalow or seaside cottage in one of the most delightful and accessible counties in Wales.

The laying out of the land as shown in the plan is a carefully considered scheme by the well known and experienced firm of Messrs. J. M. Porter & Co. of Colwyn Bay, the Surveyors and Land Agents who have had so much to do with the successful development of Colwyn Bay.

It is interesting to note that two of the lots, 3 acres each, which were immediately behind the sand dunes and the Promenade, were marketed as 'A Grand Residential Lot' and an 'Exceedingly well placed residential lot eminently adapted for the erection of one or more residences'. Had they been developed in the way intended, the area around the beach would have looked quite different. In the event, part of these lots were later acquired by the County Council and became the upper car park.

It seems that land was acquired by Charles Pozzi, a businessman and member of the Pozzi family of Bangor, jewellers. The sites were re-marketed in 1924, this time with an even glossier sales brochure. Some of the plots were bought by W. D. Williams, who developed and sold off individual sites and houses; this was the beginning of Bay View Road – a development which continued, largely to the original plan, into the 1960s and beyond.

Further along the coast, the St. David's Estate and Castle Bank were sold in 1935 and began to be developed as a camping and caravan site.

In the village itself, the area around the square also changed. The Penygroeslon cottage was demolished in the mid-1920s and the Gwynfryn Garage was built on the corner by Mrs Tryphena Jones, and run by her son Eddie Jones. Mrs Jones also donated the land behind the garage to the British Legion for the Ex-Servicemen's Hall, which was opened in 1933. As well as providing a venue for concerts and films, it also had a billiards room which was very popular with local youngsters.

A series of substantial houses were built on the road to Moelfre by David and Owen Williams, brothers who had moved back to the area having been successful as builders in Liverpool. Together with two other brothers they built Hafod, Haulfryn, Olgra, Cae Marl and Croes Allgo.

A further attraction was added to Benllech when Newsome's Fun Fair came to the village for the summer. The Newsome family arrived on Anglesey in the early 1930s and travelled to many towns and villages in North Wales, especially on Anglesey; the war years were spent mainly in Holyhead and Benllech. They purchased land at Tyn Pwll, Ty'n-y-gongl, along with a large building known as Premier Garage which adjoined the land. This was one of the places where John Newsome made and maintained the fairground equipment. The family continued to travel after the war, spending the summers in Benllech. In 1978 it was decided to close the fair at Benllech and diversify into other businesses.

One of the biggest changes in the district began when Fred Hewitt arrived in the area in the early 1920s. Originally from Ireland, he began by buying a few horses from travellers and started up a horse-riding business, taking 'picnic' rides from Benllech to Llanddona, some on a lead rein. The first customers on these rides included the Verney family from Wern-y-Wylan, the Assheton-Smiths from the Faenol Estate, and the Cadbury family from Birmingham. Fred lived with his wife Lucy in Benllech Uchaf on Beach Road and then Benllech Farm, where they kept a dairy herd, sheep and horses.

In the 1930s, a few wooden caravans started arriving on the fields, and these increased as caravanning became popular. By the end of the decade furnished caravans were being let 'spotlessly clean' for 12s 6d a week. Fred Hewitt introduced donkey-rides onto the beach and owned a stallion donkey for breeding – the donkeys would become a memorable part of family holidays at Benllech for many years. Fred and Lucy's son John inherited the business in 1958 and it has continued to be run by the family.

With the Second World War looming, Benllech had lost none of its appeal. In an article in March 1939, entitled 'In the Safety Zone', the *Liverpool Daily Post* reported:

> During the recent crisis owners of country cottages, in North Wales and elsewhere, found themselves the object of some envy by friends, while relatives made tentative inquiries as to the possibility of being accommodated should the worst come to the worst. There has always been a demand for what is known as the "week-end cottage," especially in North Wales, and particularly within easy reach of Liverpool, and there will be an opportunity to see whether the present state of affairs has caused any marked appreciation in the value of such property when four small houses in Benllech Bay, one of the most popular parts of the island of Anglesey, are offered, together with building land, by Mr G. Williams at Benllech. Wars and rumours of wars apart, cottages in favoured parts of North Wales

can nearly always be let at "seasonal" rentals during the holiday months, but the heading above certainly suggests that there is a special appeal at the present time.

Three months later, the prospect of war became even more of a reality as *HMS Thetis*, a Royal Navy submarine, sank off the North Wales coast while undergoing sea trials. 99 men died in the tragedy and only 4 survived - the Royal Navy's worst peacetime submarine disaster. The stricken vessel was eventually beached at Traeth Bychan and the bodies removed to Holyhead for burial.

Britain entered the war in September and Benllech again played its part in the war effort: many refugees from Liverpool and other cities were hosted in the community; part of the D-Day invasion fleet assembled on the beach before setting off for Normandy; and the BBC requisitioned the Wendon Café, where the popular war-time radio show ITMA featuring Tommy Handley was rehearsed and produced.

By the end of the conflict, a further thirteen names would be added to the Benllech War Memorial.

39. The Promenade and the Shell Café during the First World War

40. On the beach, 1916

41. The Benllech football team 1922/23 with Mrs Richards, Glanrafon Hotel, holding the trophy

42. Côr Bro Goronwy, 1930, with J. C. Parry the choirmaster

43. Constable Robert Pritchard and his family outside the original Minffordd farm

44. John Davies flanked by Anglesey police officers after his arrest

45. 'Happy Valley' with teas being served from the hut

46. A picnic by the Second Bay, 1930s

47. A beach scene during the 1930s

48. The Wendon Café, with cars parked on the Promenade

49. Strolling by the Glanrafon Hotel, with the tennis courts opposite

50. The Benllech bus outside Siop Ty'n-y-gongl

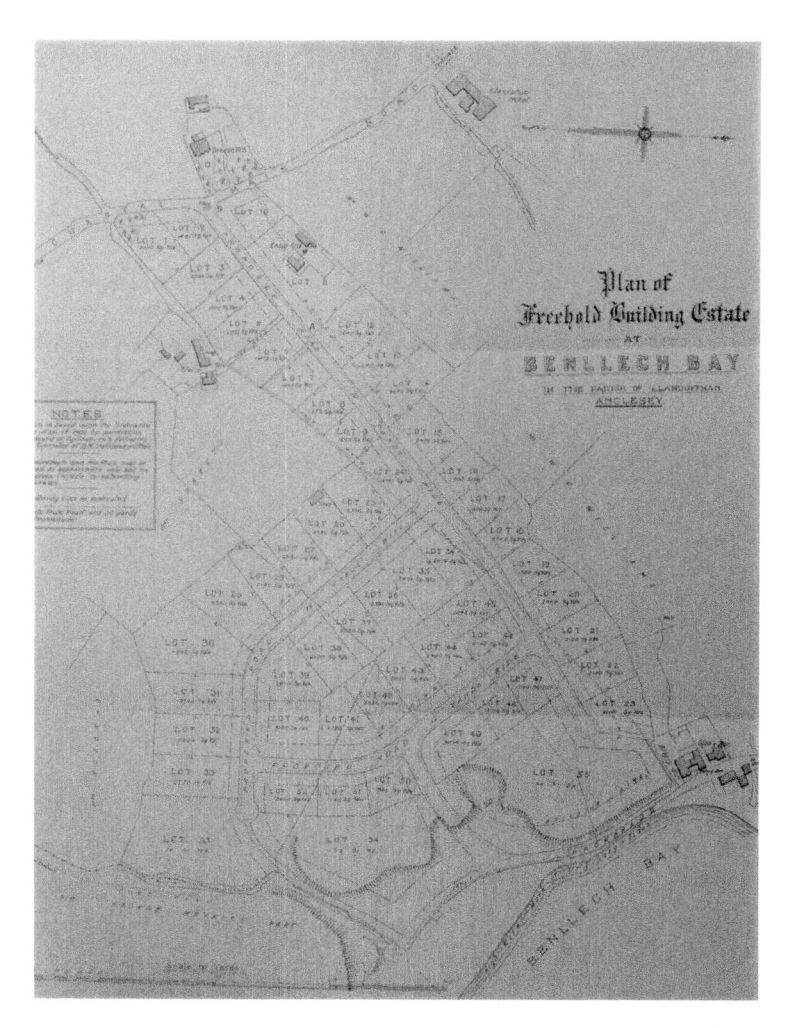

51. Plan of the Bay View development in the 1922 auction catalogue

52. Bay View Road in the 1930s

53. A view from Benllech Isaf, with herring boats in the foreground

54. Benllech square with Hewitt's riding school

55. Fred Hewitt (centre) with his donkeys

THE LEGACY

This book has primarily been about the rise of Benllech from a rural backwater 'far from everywhere of importance' at the end of the nineteenth century to become a fashionable and popular seaside village. This transformation took place gradually over several decades, and the village has continued to grow in population, driven by the building of several housing estates and the popularity of the area for static caravans, second-homes and retirement in particular. Although the social profile of the area has changed a great deal since the nineteenth century, the appearance of the beach and the centre of the village has hardly altered, and the houses and shops which were built during the earlier period continue to define the locality.

The first housing estate that was established in Benllech following the war was the Garreglwyd Estate, designed by architects Colwyn Foulkes and built by Emrys Griffith in 1952; the semi-detached houses were sold for £2,500 each. Immediately prior to the building, the Anglesey Eisteddfod was held on the fields; the first house on the estate was called *Swn y Gân* (Sound of the song) in recognition of the event.

Emrys Griffith would go on to build the first wave of bungalow housing in the village, including the Breeze Hill estate (which won a Civic Trust award), Bay View, Rhianfa and Mynachlog (Craig-y-Don). From the 1960s onwards Sam and Arthur Jones built the Maes Llydan, Fferam and Minffordd estates, and other housing has followed including Bryn Siriol and Tyddyn Fadog. It is pleasing to note that most of the estates have retained the names of the original farms on which they were built.

One of the landmark buildings in Benllech, the Glanrafon Hotel, was demolished in 2016, having served holidaymakers and locals for over a century and a quarter. At the time of writing, the old Ty'n-y-gongl school was being offered for sale as living accommodation, and the Tabernacl Chapel was being converted into a house.

There remains a strong cultural tradition in the area and *Cymdeithas Lenyddol Bro Goronwy,* the Literary Society formed in 1901, continues to this day. The Society was instrumental in raising funds for *Neuadd Goffa Goronwy Owen* (The Goronwy Owen Memorial Hall) which was opened in 1959 and which previously served as the village library.

The population of the Benllech district is now approaching 4,000 people and it is the fifth largest settlement on the island.

It has come a long way from the 'poor straggling village' which George Borrow described in the 1850s.

56. Garreglwyd Estate during the 1963 snow, looking towards Fferam

57. The author enjoying a ride at Newsome's Fun Fair, early 1960s

BIBLIOGRAPHY

Books

George Borrow, *Wild Wales: Its People, Language and Scenery* (1854).

A. D. Carr, *Medieval Anglesey,* second edition (Llangefni, 2011).

Glenda Carr, *Hen Enwau o Ynys Môn* (Caernarfon, 2015).

John Cowell, *Edwardian Anglesey – A Pictorial History*, vols. 1 and 2 (Llangefni, 1991 & 1992).

Aled Eames, *Ships and Seamen of Anglesey 1558-1918*, second edition (Llanrwst, 2011).

Aled Eames, *Meistri'r Moroedd* (Denbigh, 1978).

Gillian Hodkinson, *Lest We Forget – the Lads of Llaneugrad & Llanallgo in World War I* (2019).

Geraint Jones, *Anglesey at War* (Stroud, 2012).

Robin Evans, *Ffarwel i'r Grassholm Gribog: Moelfre a'r Môr* (Llanrwst, 2009).

R. Tudur Jones, *Tân ar yr Ynys* (Caernarfon, 2004).

J. R. Jones, *The Welsh Builder on Merseyside: Annals and Lives* (1946).

Frances Lynch, *Prehistoric Anglesey*, second edition (Llangefni, 1970).

Angharad Llwyd, *A History of the Island of Mona or Anglesey* (Ruthin, 1833).

Hywel Wyn Owen and Richard Morgan, *Dictionary of Place-names of Wales* (Llandysul, 2007).

David A. Pretty, *Two Centuries of Anglesey Schools* (Llangefni, 1977).

David A. Pretty, *Anglesey, The Concise History* (Cardiff, 2005)

David A. Pretty, *Farmer, Solidier and Politician – The Life of Brigadier-General Sir Owen Thomas, MP* (Wrexham, 2011).

W. G. Rear, *Anglesey Branch Lines – Amlwch and Red Wharf Bay* (Stockport, 1994).

Mark Redknap, *Vikings in Wales* (Cardiff, 2000).

Melville Richards (ed.), *Atlas Môn* (Llangefni, 1982).

Emyr Roberts, *Bro Goronwy: Hanes Plwyf Llanfairmathafarneithaf 1870-1914* (Llanrwst, 2019).

Jane L. Robinson, *Benllech and its Surrounding Parish of Llanfair Mathafarn Eithaf* (Wrexham, 1993).

Mike Smylie, *Anglesey and its Coastal Tradition* (Llanrwst, 2000).

Mike Smylie, *The Herring Fishers of Wales* (Llanrwst, 1998).

Siân Williams, *Mat Racs* (Caernarfon, 1983).

Articles

C. W. Phillips, 'The excavation of a hut group at Pant-y-Saer in the parish of Llanfair-Mathafarn- Eithaf, Anglesey', *Archaeologia Cambrensis* (1934), pp. 1-36.

Emyr Roberts, 'Through stormy weather – the struggle to establish the Tabernacl Board School, Ty'nygongl', *Transactions of the Anglesey Antiquarian Society* (2019), pp. 75-87.

Various newspapers of the period were consulted, in particular *The North Wales Chronicle*, *Y Clorianydd*, and the *Carnarvon and Denbigh Herald.*

Historical documents held at the Anglesey Archives, the Bangor University Archives, the National Library of Wales, and the National Archives were also used.

Local sources, in particular *Yr Arwydd* and Benllech Web, were invaluable.

Printed in Great Britain
by Amazon